MAGNUS™
ROBOT FIGHTER 1

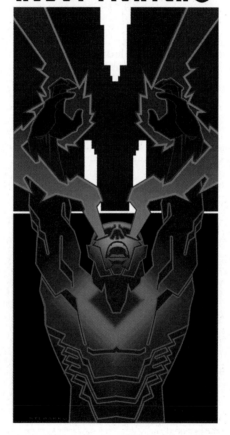

MAGNUS
ROBOT FIGHTER ①

PAST AND PRESENT

ONE THOUSAND YEARS AGO . . .

. . . The Traffickers, an alien race of cyborg pirate-entrepreneurs, secretly sent robots disguised as men to corrupt humanity's robot servants and incite wars among the nations and between man and machine. Then, in the wake of those devastating conflicts, the Traffickers loosed nanobots, microscopic machines, to activate dormant volcanoes and melt Earth's ice caps. But, before Earth's biosphere could completely destabilize and render humanity helpless, the peoples of Earth recognized and repelled their true enemy. Unfortunately, worldwide weather patterns were left in chaos and, within a generation, massive storms toppled the Earth into a bleak and terrible ice age. At first, as technological civilization deteriorated, humanity began a breeding program focused on developing telepathy, telekinesis and other mental abilities. But soon, memories of the Trafficker War receded, and impatient humanity began to recreate complex machines. They constructed weather stations which sent electromagnetic pulses into the atmosphere to disrupt the ever-threatening storm systems. And, once again, they built robots to serve humanity.

But, cautioned by their experience with the Traffickers, they made laws to regulate robot forms: robots must look like machines, they must be easily visible to the naked human eye, and the creation of Cyborgs in any form was forbidden. The robots' programming, too, was carefully controlled. Robots were forbidden to injure a human through action or inaction. Where possible, they must obey orders given by humans and protect their own existence. To guard and serve humanity would be their primary function. In time, humanity placed great faith in these mechanical paragons, and ceded to them augmented responsibilities. And a new golden age of peace and prosperity was born on Earth.

TWENTY-FIVE YEARS AGO . . .

. . .1A, an ancient robot who had survived the earlier cycle of destruction, became convinced that trouble was imminent. He feared that humans, with the connivance of robots acting in what they perceived as humanity's best interest, had allowed themselves to grow soft. And that robots, with the best of programmed motives, would continue to keep them that way. 1A took an orphaned human infant to a laboratory deep beneath the sea. As the child grew to manhood, 1A educated him in all human knowledge, honed his body to superior quickness and strength, taught him ancient forms of combat, and inculcated in him the virtues of honesty, diligence, fidelity and courage. He also implanted a device into his skull that allowed him to eavesdrop on robot conversations and taught him to toughen his skin at will to a steel-like hardness.

FIVE YEARS AGO . . .

. . . Magnus arrived in the North Am megalopolis. His mission was straightforward—to combat evil robots wherever they appeared. That his arrival coincided with the appearance of many varieties of evil robot was lost on most of humanity. What they noticed was that Magnus heroically vanquished them all. Magnus won the heart of Leeja Clane, a budding telepath, the beautiful young daughter of Senator Zeramiah Clane. And Magnus became North Am's champion.

SIX WEEKS AGO . . .

. . . the Traffickers began a second attempt at the hostile takeover of the Earth. The alien cyborgs battered North Am's weather stations until only Central Sector Weather Control remained fully operational. They pounded North Am's power grid, reducing energy output. Energy was shunted from other processes to shore up the anti-grav units that supported the mile-high megalopolis and scientists hastily constructed force-fields to protect valuable power stations from Trafficker attack. In the Capitol region, the senate met to consider North Am's options. While overhead, the Traffickers prepared for their final assault . . .

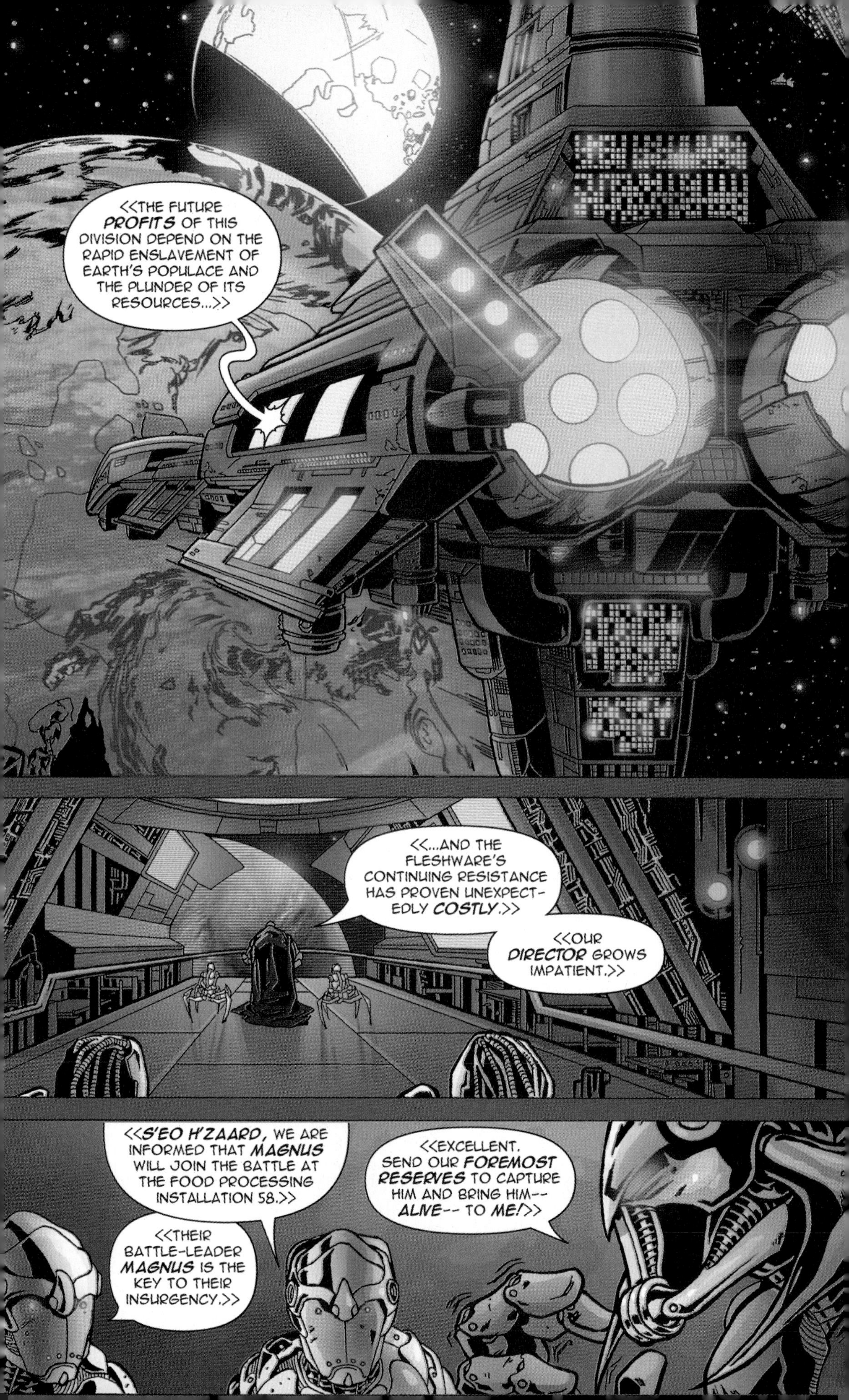
<<THE FUTURE PROFITS OF THIS DIVISION DEPEND ON THE RAPID ENSLAVEMENT OF EARTH'S POPULACE AND THE PLUNDER OF ITS RESOURCES...>>
<<...AND THE FLESHWARE'S CONTINUING RESISTANCE HAS PROVEN UNEXPECTEDLY COSTLY.>>
<<OUR DIRECTOR GROWS IMPATIENT.>>
<<S'EO H'ZAARD, WE ARE INFORMED THAT MAGNUS WILL JOIN THE BATTLE AT THE FOOD PROCESSING INSTALLATION 58.>>
<<THEIR BATTLE-LEADER MAGNUS IS THE KEY TO THEIR INSURGENCY.>>
<<EXCELLENT. SEND OUR FOREMOST RESERVES TO CAPTURE HIM AND BRING HIM-- ALIVE-- TO ME!>>

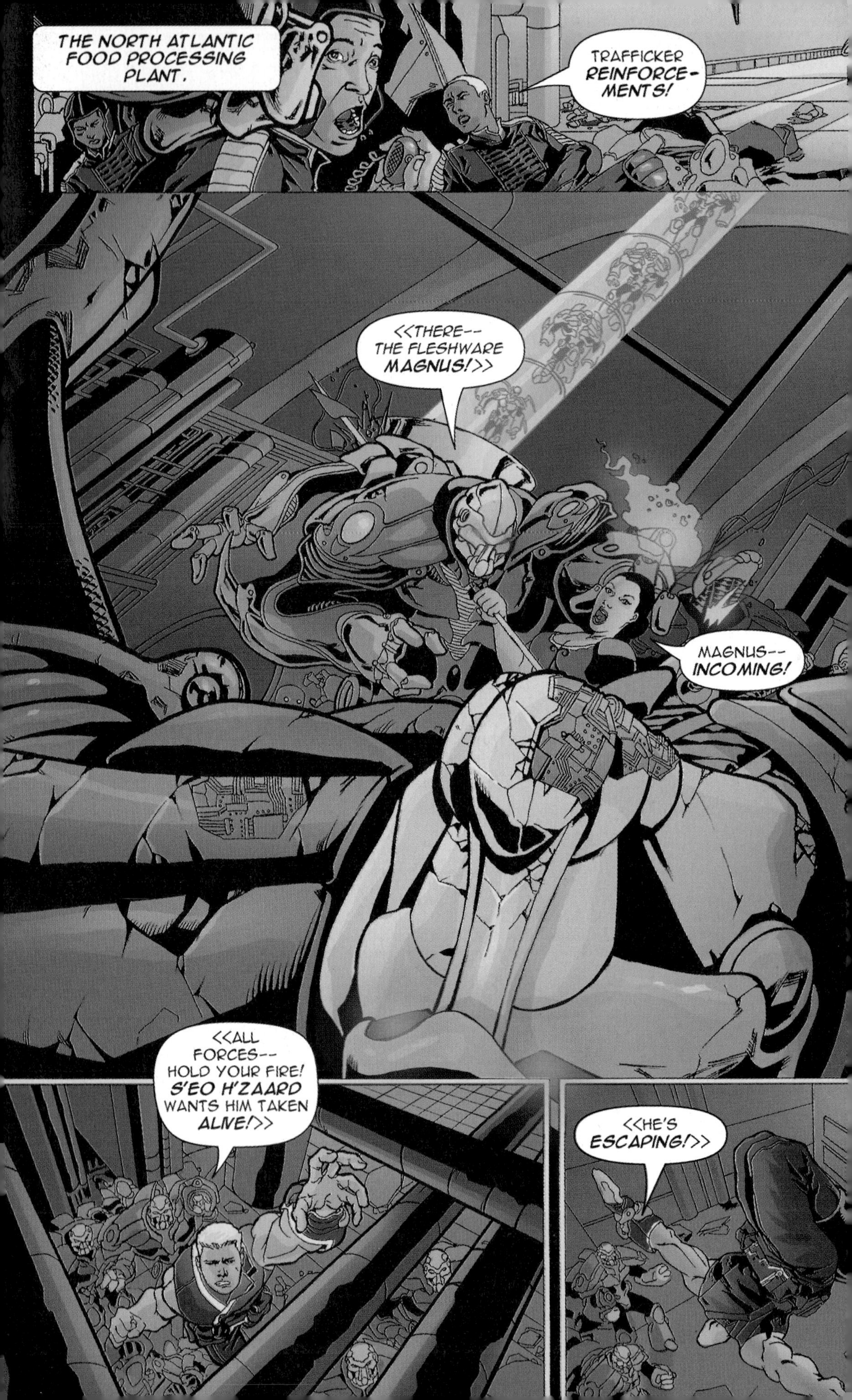
THE NORTH ATLANTIC FOOD PROCESSING PLANT.
TRAFFICKER REINFORCE-MENTS!
<<THERE-- THE FLESHWARE MAGNUS!>>
MAGNUS-- INCOMING!
<<ALL FORCES-- HOLD YOUR FIRE! S'EO H'ZAARD WANTS HIM TAKEN ALIVE!>>
<<HE'S ESCAPING!>>

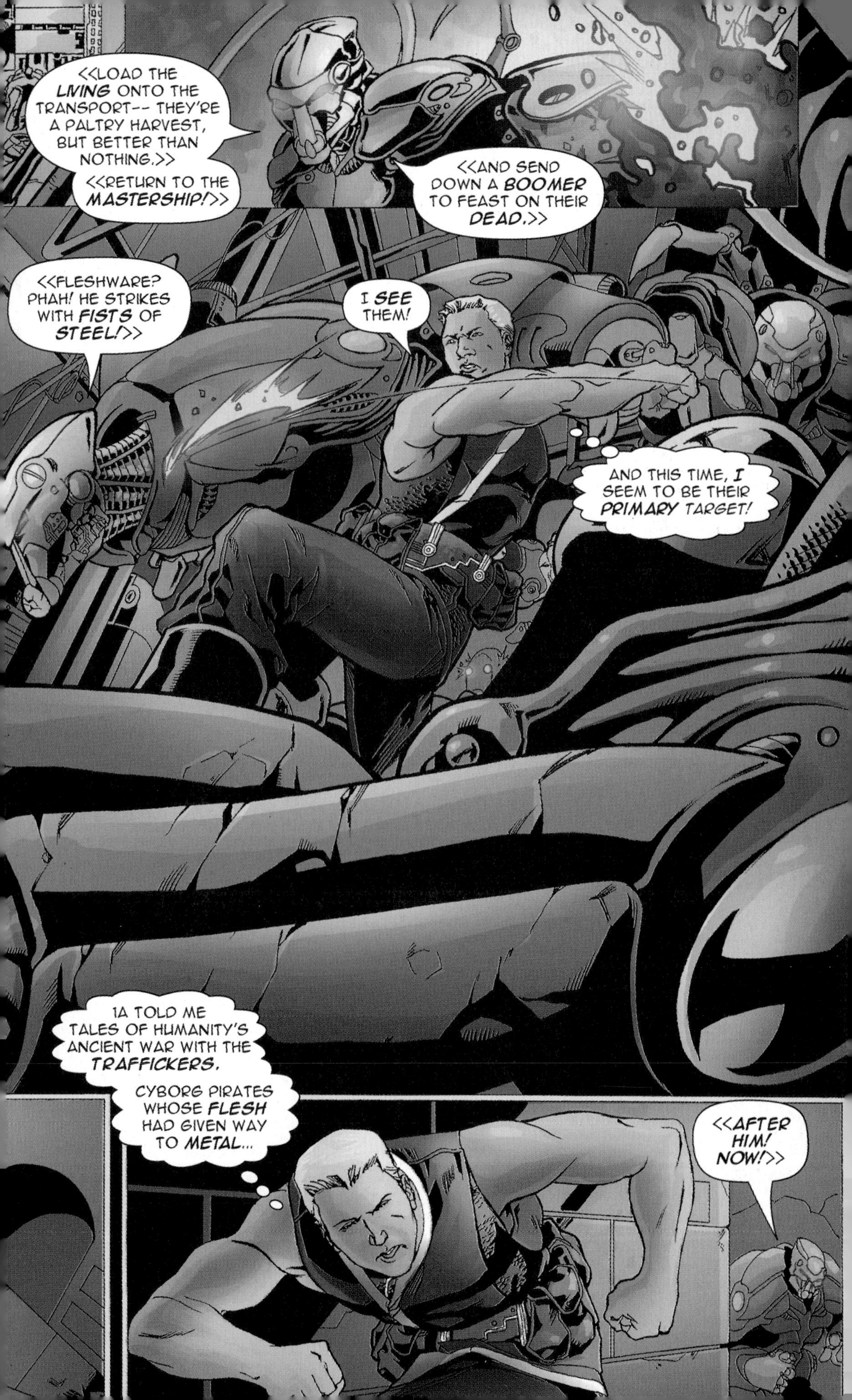

<<LOAD THE LIVING ONTO THE TRANSPORT-- THEY'RE A PALTRY HARVEST, BUT BETTER THAN NOTHING.>>
<<RETURN TO THE MASTERSHIP!>>
<<AND SEND DOWN A BOOMER TO FEAST ON THEIR DEAD.>>
<<FLESHWARE? PHAH! HE STRIKES WITH FISTS OF STEEL!>>
I SEE THEM!
AND THIS TIME, I SEEM TO BE THEIR PRIMARY TARGET!
1A TOLD ME TALES OF HUMANITY'S ANCIENT WAR WITH THE TRAFFICKERS.
CYBORG PIRATES WHOSE FLESH HAD GIVEN WAY TO METAL...
<<AFTER HIM! NOW!>>

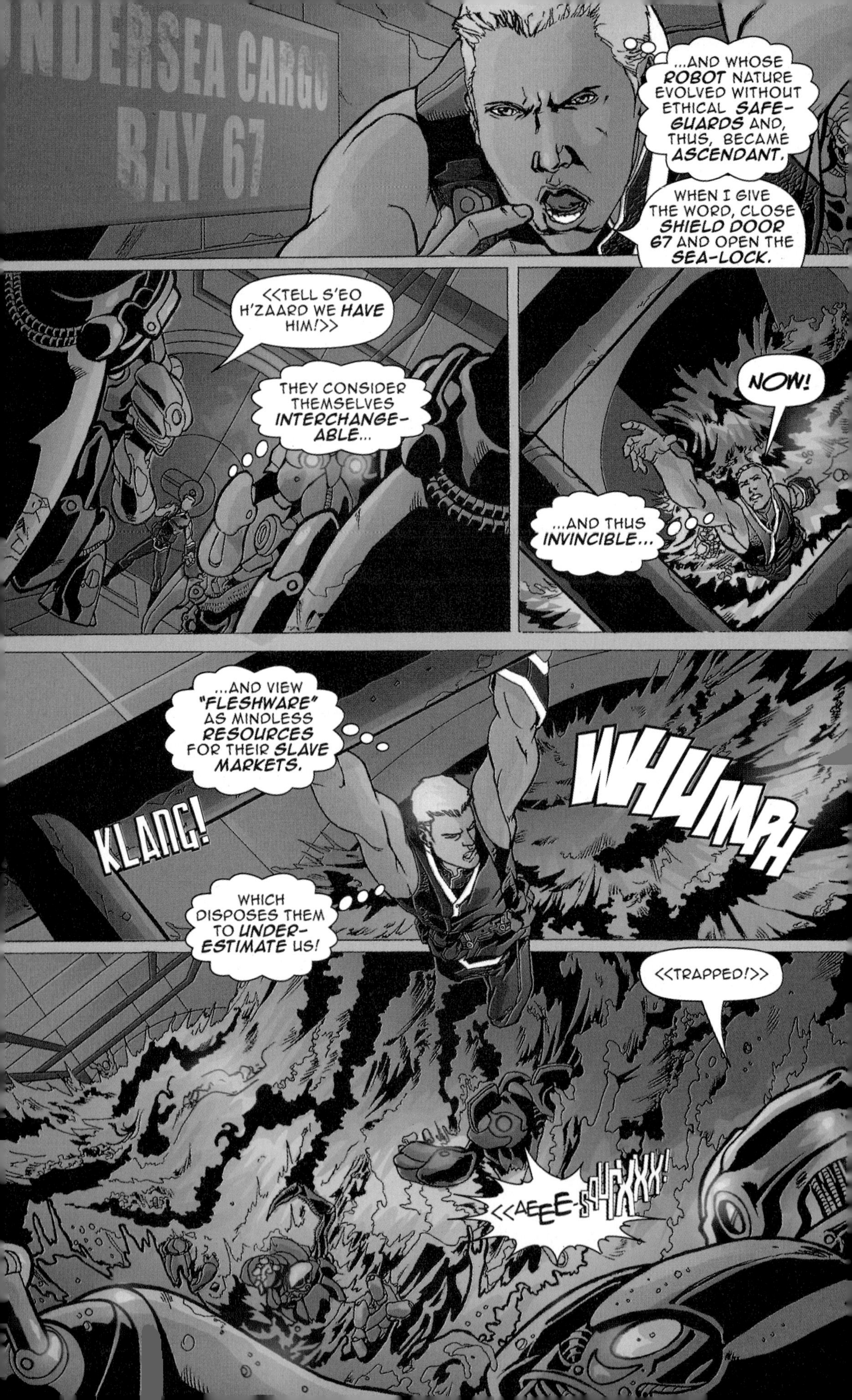
UNDERSEA CARGO BAY 67
...AND WHOSE ROBOT NATURE EVOLVED WITHOUT ETHICAL SAFE-GUARDS AND, THUS, BECAME ASCENDANT.
WHEN I GIVE THE WORD, CLOSE SHIELD DOOR 67 AND OPEN THE SEA-LOCK.
<<TELL S'EO H'ZAARD WE HAVE HIM!>>
THEY CONSIDER THEMSELVES INTERCHANGE-ABLE...
NOW!
...AND THUS INVINCIBLE...
...AND VIEW "FLESHWARE" AS MINDLESS RESOURCES FOR THEIR SLAVE MARKETS.
WHUMPH
KLANG!
WHICH DISPOSES THEM TO UNDER-ESTIMATE US!
<<TRAPPED!>>

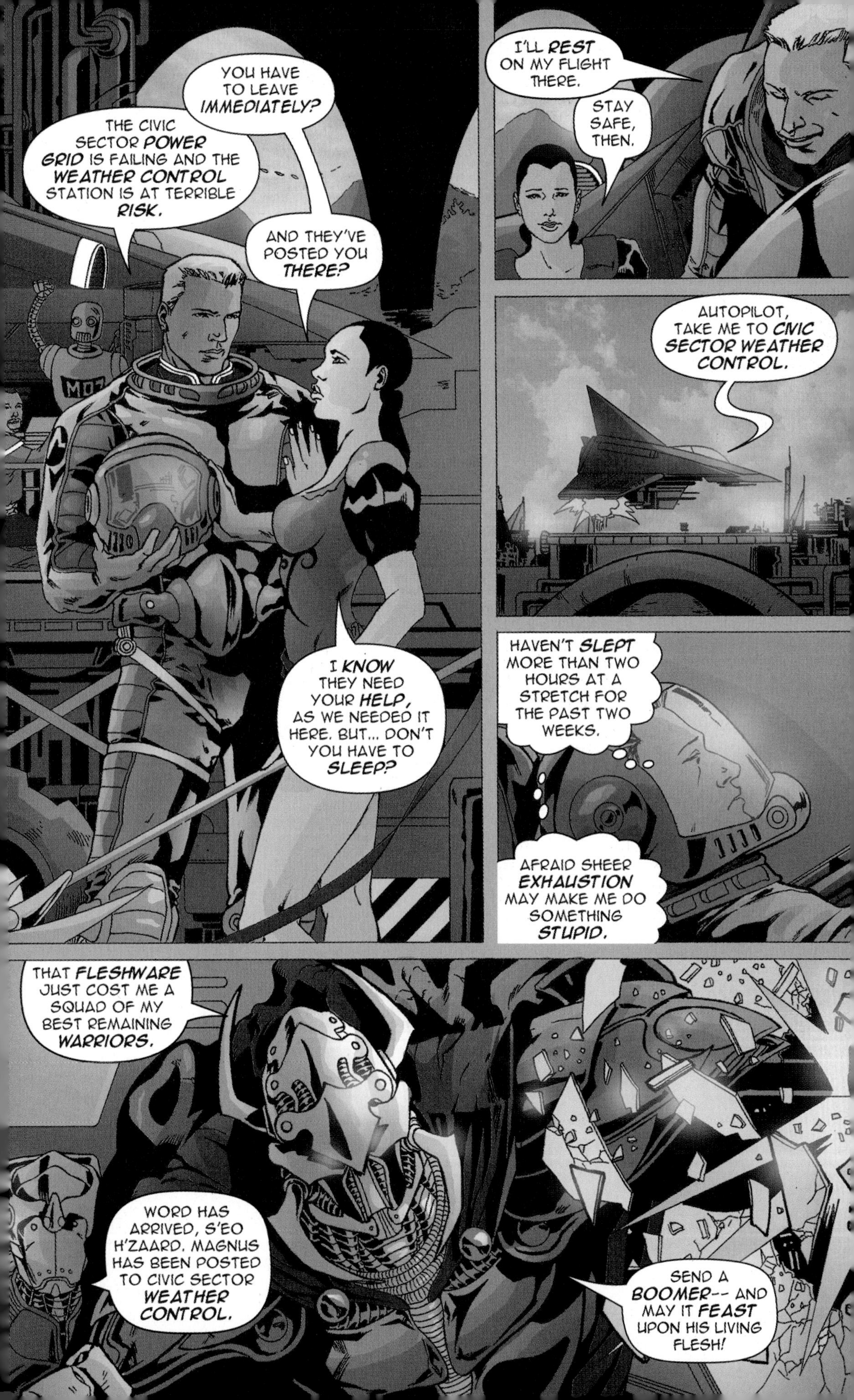
THE CIVIC SECTOR POWER GRID IS FAILING AND THE WEATHER CONTROL STATION IS AT TERRIBLE RISK.
YOU HAVE TO LEAVE IMMEDIATELY?
AND THEY'VE POSTED YOU THERE?
MO7
I KNOW THEY NEED YOUR HELP, AS WE NEEDED IT HERE. BUT... DON'T YOU HAVE TO SLEEP?
I'LL REST ON MY FLIGHT THERE.
STAY SAFE, THEN.
AUTOPILOT, TAKE ME TO CIVIC SECTOR WEATHER CONTROL.
HAVEN'T SLEPT MORE THAN TWO HOURS AT A STRETCH FOR THE PAST TWO WEEKS.
AFRAID SHEER EXHAUSTION MAY MAKE ME DO SOMETHING STUPID.
THAT FLESHWARE JUST COST ME A SQUAD OF MY BEST REMAINING WARRIORS.
WORD HAS ARRIVED, S'EO H'ZAARD. MAGNUS HAS BEEN POSTED TO CIVIC SECTOR WEATHER CONTROL.
SEND A BOOMER-- AND MAY IT FEAST UPON HIS LIVING FLESH!

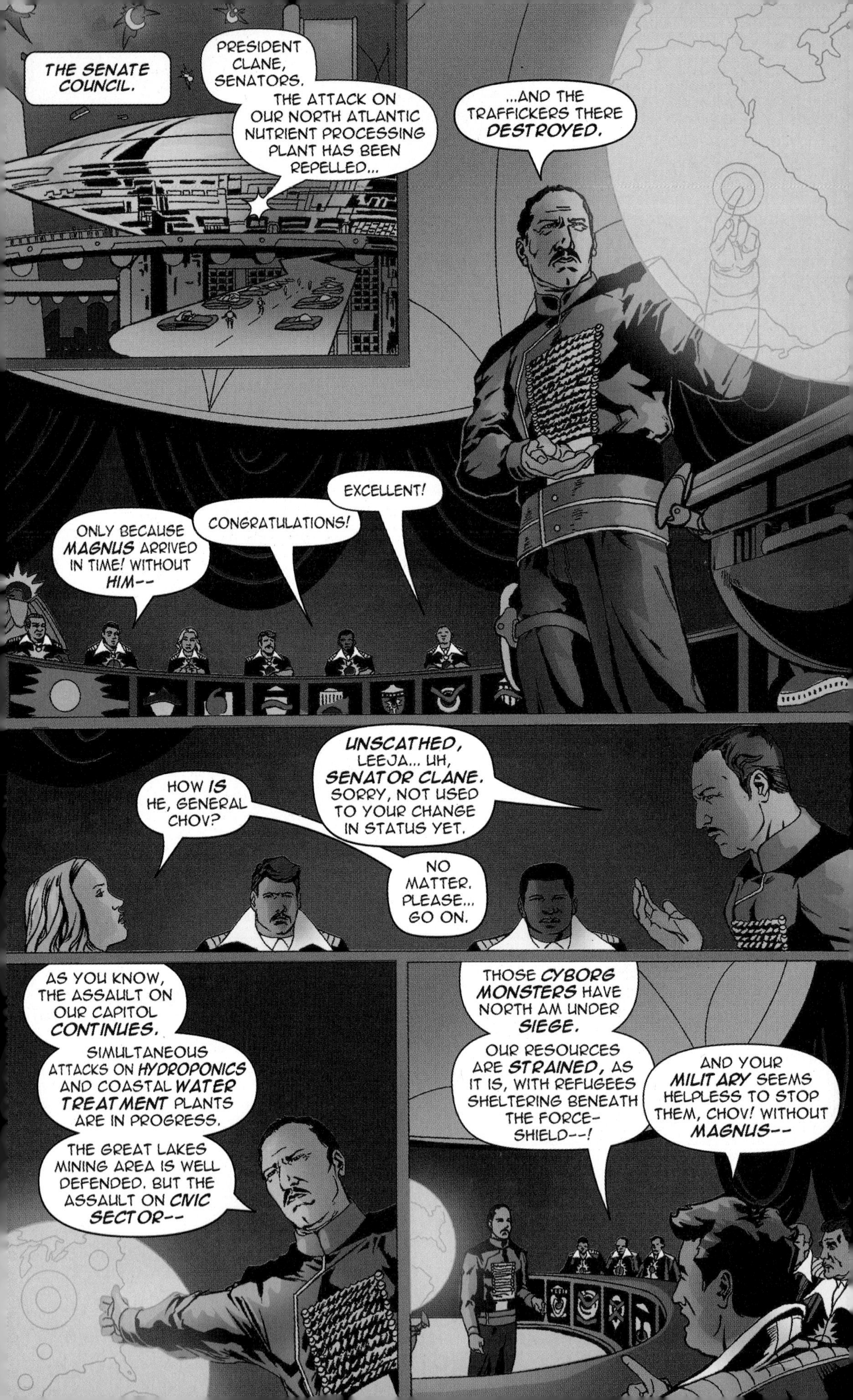
THE SENATE COUNCIL.
PRESIDENT CLANE, SENATORS.
THE ATTACK ON OUR NORTH ATLANTIC NUTRIENT PROCESSING PLANT HAS BEEN REPELLED...
...AND THE TRAFFICKERS THERE DESTROYED.
ONLY BECAUSE MAGNUS ARRIVED IN TIME! WITHOUT HIM--
CONGRATULATIONS!
EXCELLENT!
HOW IS HE, GENERAL CHOV?
UNSCATHED, LEEJA... UH, SENATOR CLANE. SORRY, NOT USED TO YOUR CHANGE IN STATUS YET.
NO MATTER. PLEASE... GO ON.
AS YOU KNOW, THE ASSAULT ON OUR CAPITOL CONTINUES.
SIMULTANEOUS ATTACKS ON HYDROPONICS AND COASTAL WATER TREATMENT PLANTS ARE IN PROGRESS.
THE GREAT LAKES MINING AREA IS WELL DEFENDED. BUT THE ASSAULT ON CIVIC SECTOR--
THOSE CYBORG MONSTERS HAVE NORTH AM UNDER SIEGE.
OUR RESOURCES ARE STRAINED, AS IT IS, WITH REFUGEES SHELTERING BENEATH THE FORCE-SHIELD--!
AND YOUR MILITARY SEEMS HELPLESS TO STOP THEM, CHOV! WITHOUT MAGNUS--

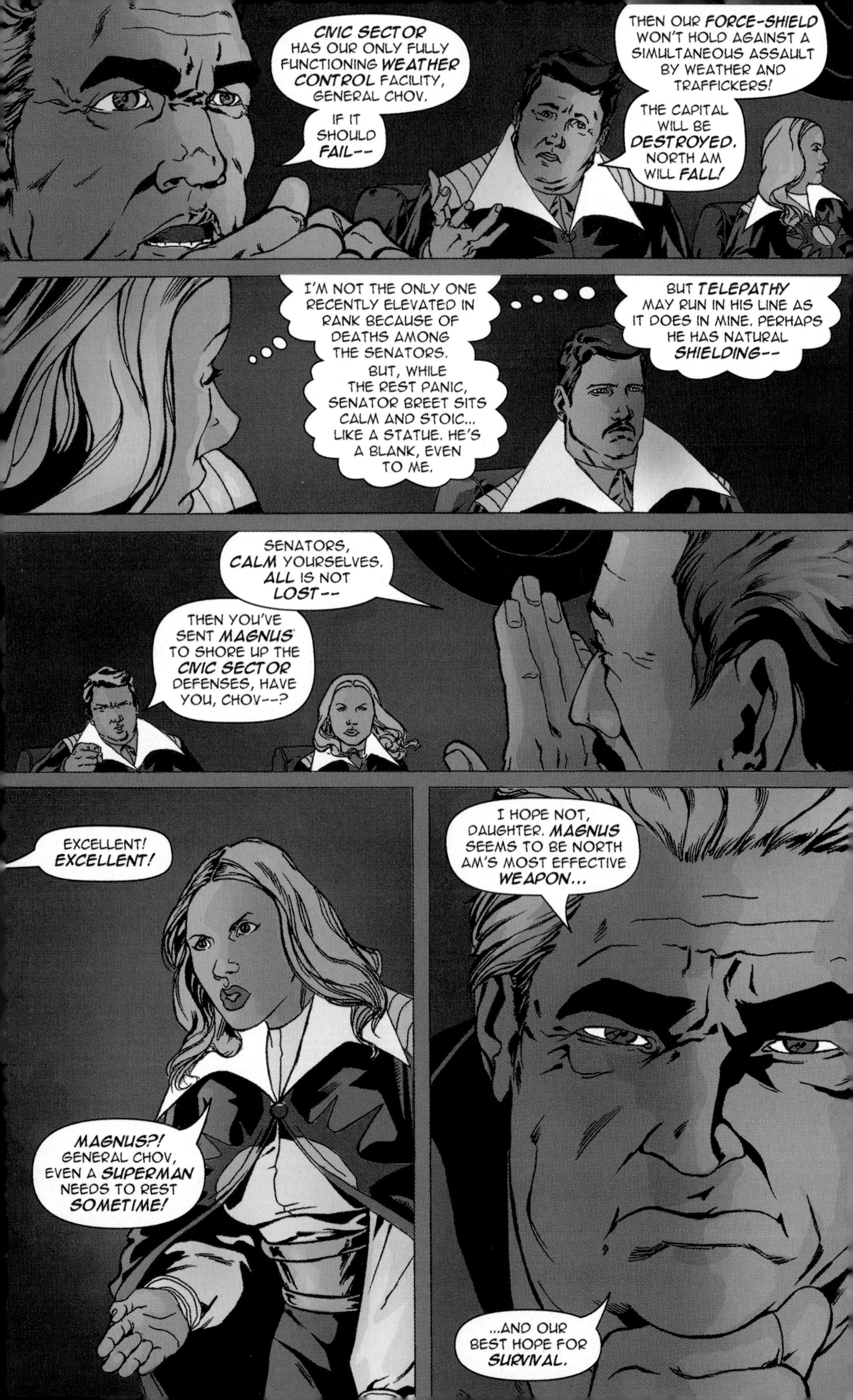
CIVIC SECTOR HAS OUR ONLY FULLY FUNCTIONING WEATHER CONTROL FACILITY, GENERAL CHOV.
IF IT SHOULD FAIL--
THEN OUR FORCE-SHIELD WON'T HOLD AGAINST A SIMULTANEOUS ASSAULT BY WEATHER AND TRAFFICKERS!
THE CAPITAL WILL BE DESTROYED. NORTH AM WILL FALL!
I'M NOT THE ONLY ONE RECENTLY ELEVATED IN RANK BECAUSE OF DEATHS AMONG THE SENATORS.
BUT, WHILE THE REST PANIC, SENATOR BREET SITS CALM AND STOIC... LIKE A STATUE. HE'S A BLANK, EVEN TO ME.
BUT TELEPATHY MAY RUN IN HIS LINE AS IT DOES IN MINE. PERHAPS HE HAS NATURAL SHIELDING--
SENATORS, CALM YOURSELVES. ALL IS NOT LOST--
THEN YOU'VE SENT MAGNUS TO SHORE UP THE CIVIC SECTOR DEFENSES, HAVE YOU, CHOV--?
EXCELLENT! EXCELLENT!
MAGNUS?! GENERAL CHOV, EVEN A SUPERMAN NEEDS TO REST SOMETIME!
I HOPE NOT, DAUGHTER. MAGNUS SEEMS TO BE NORTH AM'S MOST EFFECTIVE WEAPON...
...AND OUR BEST HOPE FOR SURVIVAL.

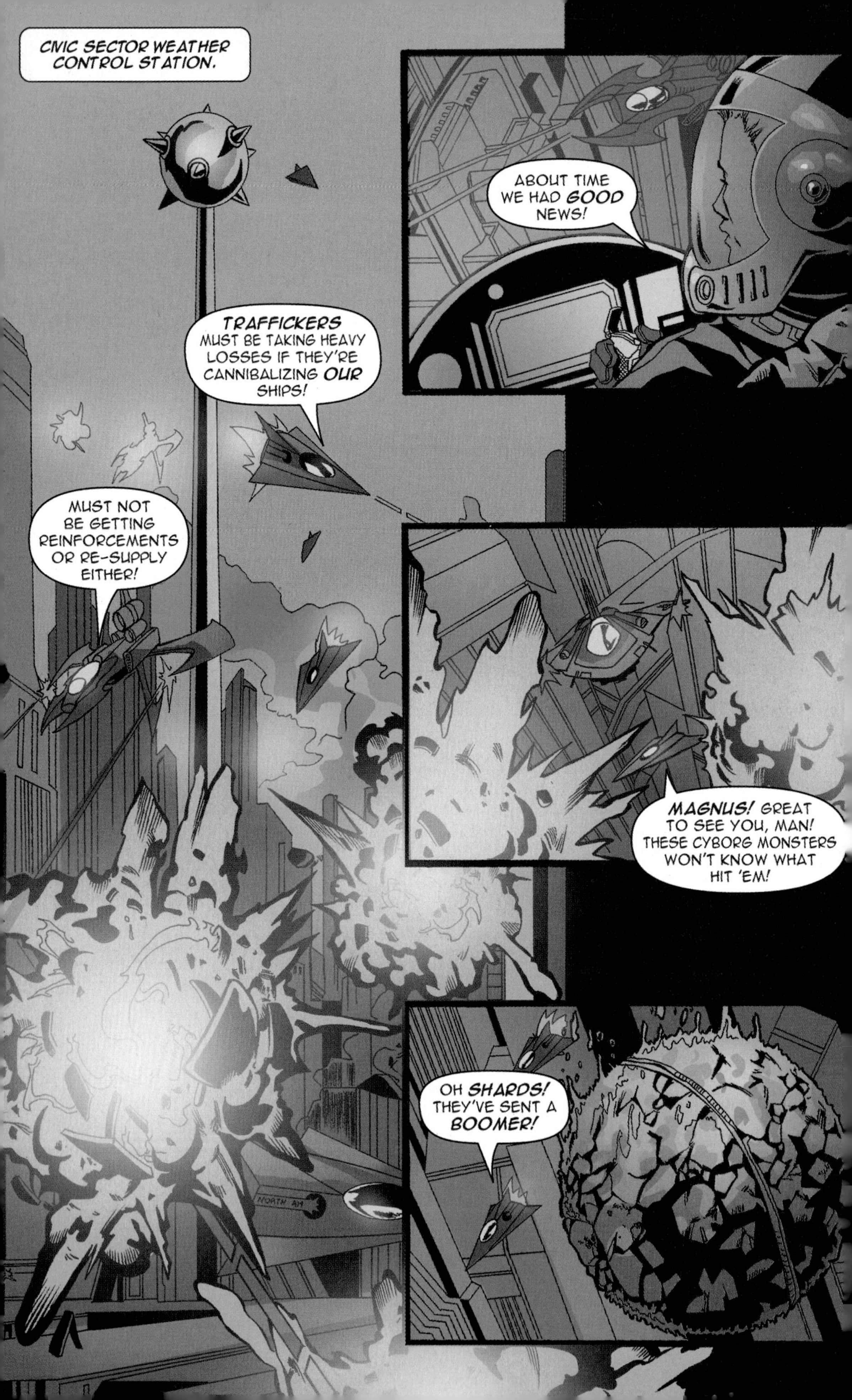
CIVIC SECTOR WEATHER CONTROL STATION.
ABOUT TIME WE HAD GOOD NEWS!
TRAFFICKERS MUST BE TAKING HEAVY LOSSES IF THEY'RE CANNIBALIZING OUR SHIPS!
MUST NOT BE GETTING REINFORCEMENTS OR RE-SUPPLY EITHER!
MAGNUS! GREAT TO SEE YOU, MAN! THESE CYBORG MONSTERS WON'T KNOW WHAT HIT 'EM!
OH SHARDS! THEY'VE SENT A BOOMER!
NORTH AM

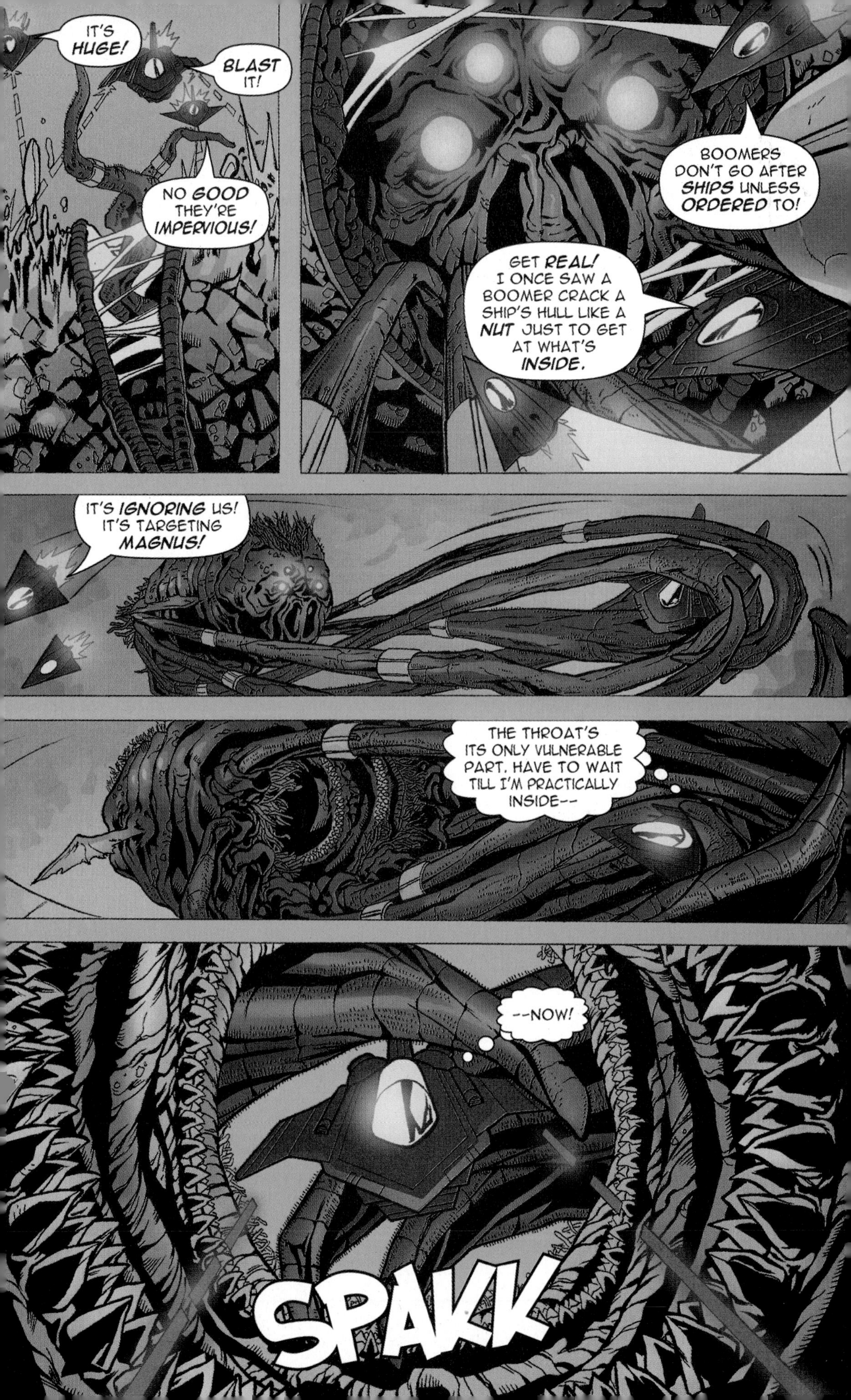
IT'S HUGE!
BLAST IT!
NO GOOD THEY'RE IMPERVIOUS!
BOOMERS DON'T GO AFTER SHIPS UNLESS ORDERED TO!
GET REAL! I ONCE SAW A BOOMER CRACK A SHIP'S HULL LIKE A NUT JUST TO GET AT WHAT'S INSIDE.
IT'S IGNORING US! IT'S TARGETING MAGNUS!
THE THROAT'S ITS ONLY VULNERABLE PART. HAVE TO WAIT TILL I'M PRACTICALLY INSIDE--
--NOW!
SPAKK

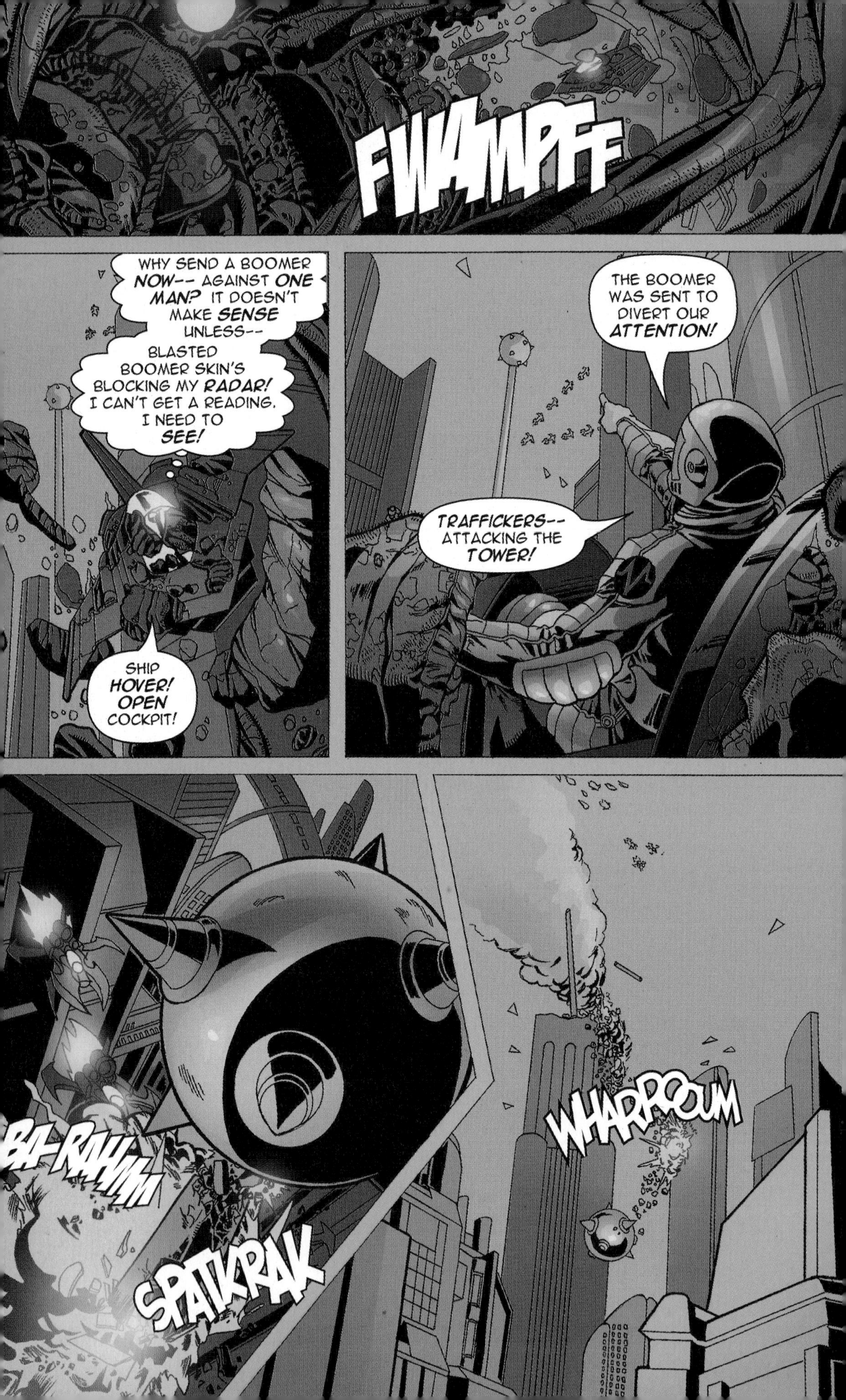
FWAMPFF
WHY SEND A BOOMER NOW-- AGAINST ONE MAN? IT DOESN'T MAKE SENSE UNLESS--
BLASTED BOOMER SKIN'S BLOCKING MY RADAR! I CAN'T GET A READING. I NEED TO SEE!
SHIP HOVER! OPEN COCKPIT!
THE BOOMER WAS SENT TO DIVERT OUR ATTENTION!
TRAFFICKERS-- ATTACKING THE TOWER!
BA-RAHMM
SPATKRAK
WHARROOUM

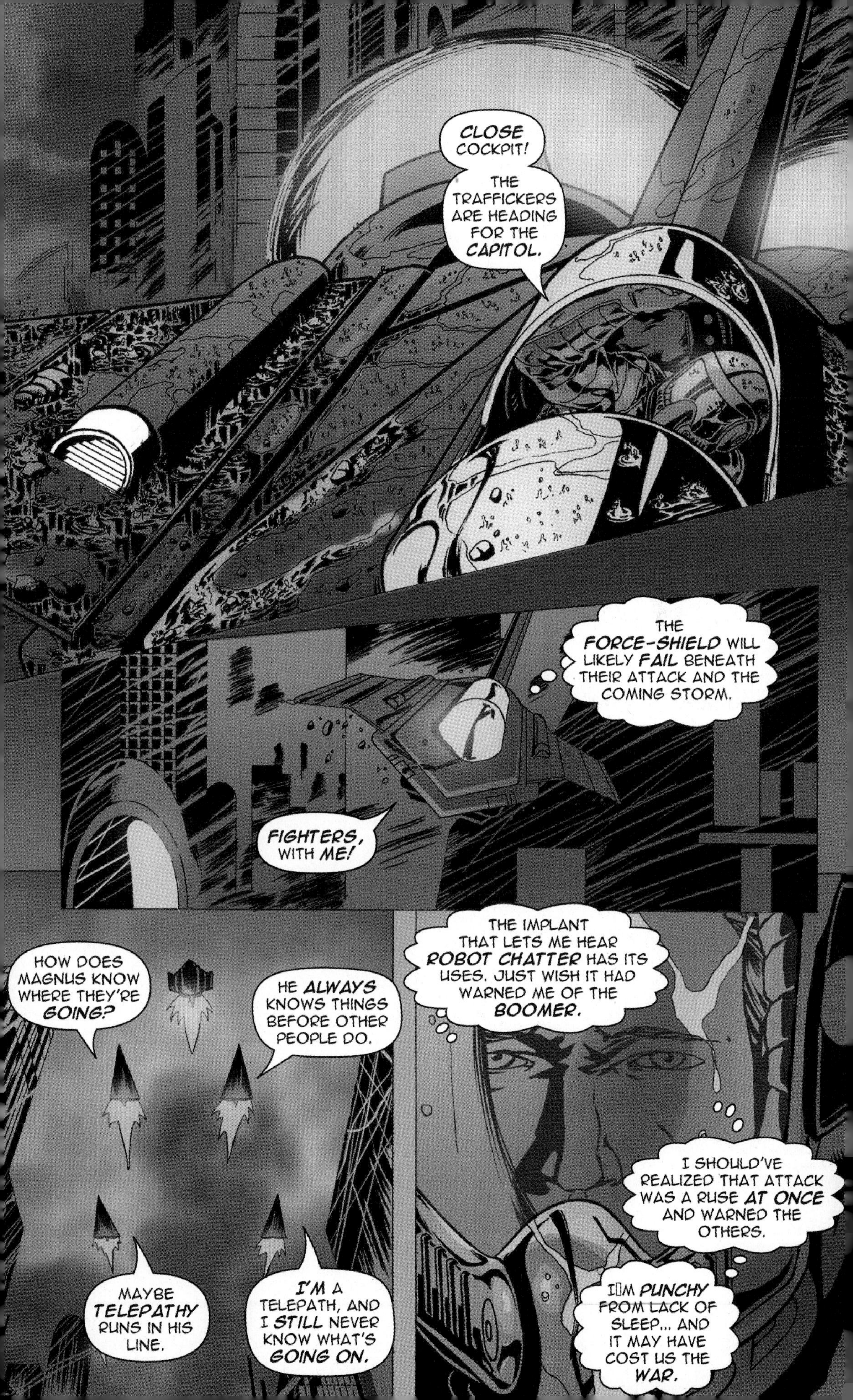
CLOSE COCKPIT!
THE TRAFFICKERS ARE HEADING FOR THE CAPITOL.
THE FORCE-SHIELD WILL LIKELY FAIL BENEATH THEIR ATTACK AND THE COMING STORM.
FIGHTERS, WITH ME!
HOW DOES MAGNUS KNOW WHERE THEY'RE GOING?
HE ALWAYS KNOWS THINGS BEFORE OTHER PEOPLE DO.
MAYBE TELEPATHY RUNS IN HIS LINE.
I'M A TELEPATH, AND I STILL NEVER KNOW WHAT'S GOING ON.
THE IMPLANT THAT LETS ME HEAR ROBOT CHATTER HAS ITS USES. JUST WISH IT HAD WARNED ME OF THE BOOMER.
I SHOULD'VE REALIZED THAT ATTACK WAS A RUSE AT ONCE AND WARNED THE OTHERS.
I'M PUNCHY FROM LACK OF SLEEP... AND IT MAY HAVE COST US THE WAR.

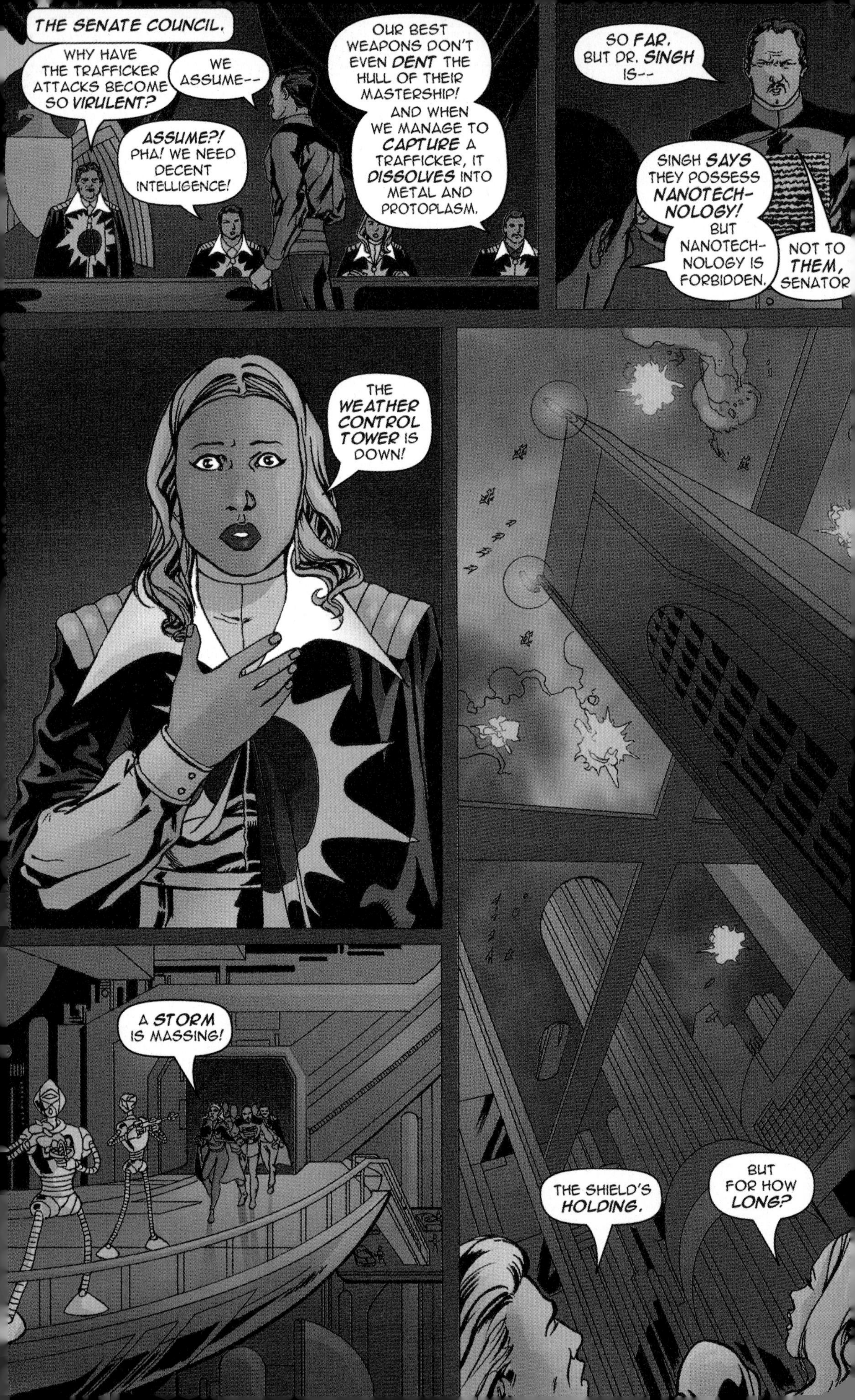
THE SENATE COUNCIL.
WHY HAVE THE TRAFFICKER ATTACKS BECOME SO VIRULENT?
WE ASSUME--
ASSUME?! PHA! WE NEED DECENT INTELLIGENCE!
OUR BEST WEAPONS DON'T EVEN DENT THE HULL OF THEIR MASTERSHIP!
AND WHEN WE MANAGE TO CAPTURE A TRAFFICKER, IT DISSOLVES INTO METAL AND PROTOPLASM.
SO FAR. BUT DR. SINGH IS--
SINGH SAYS THEY POSSESS NANOTECHNOLOGY!
BUT NANOTECHNOLOGY IS FORBIDDEN.
NOT TO THEM, SENATOR
THE WEATHER CONTROL TOWER IS DOWN!
A STORM IS MASSING!
THE SHIELD'S HOLDING.
BUT FOR HOW LONG?

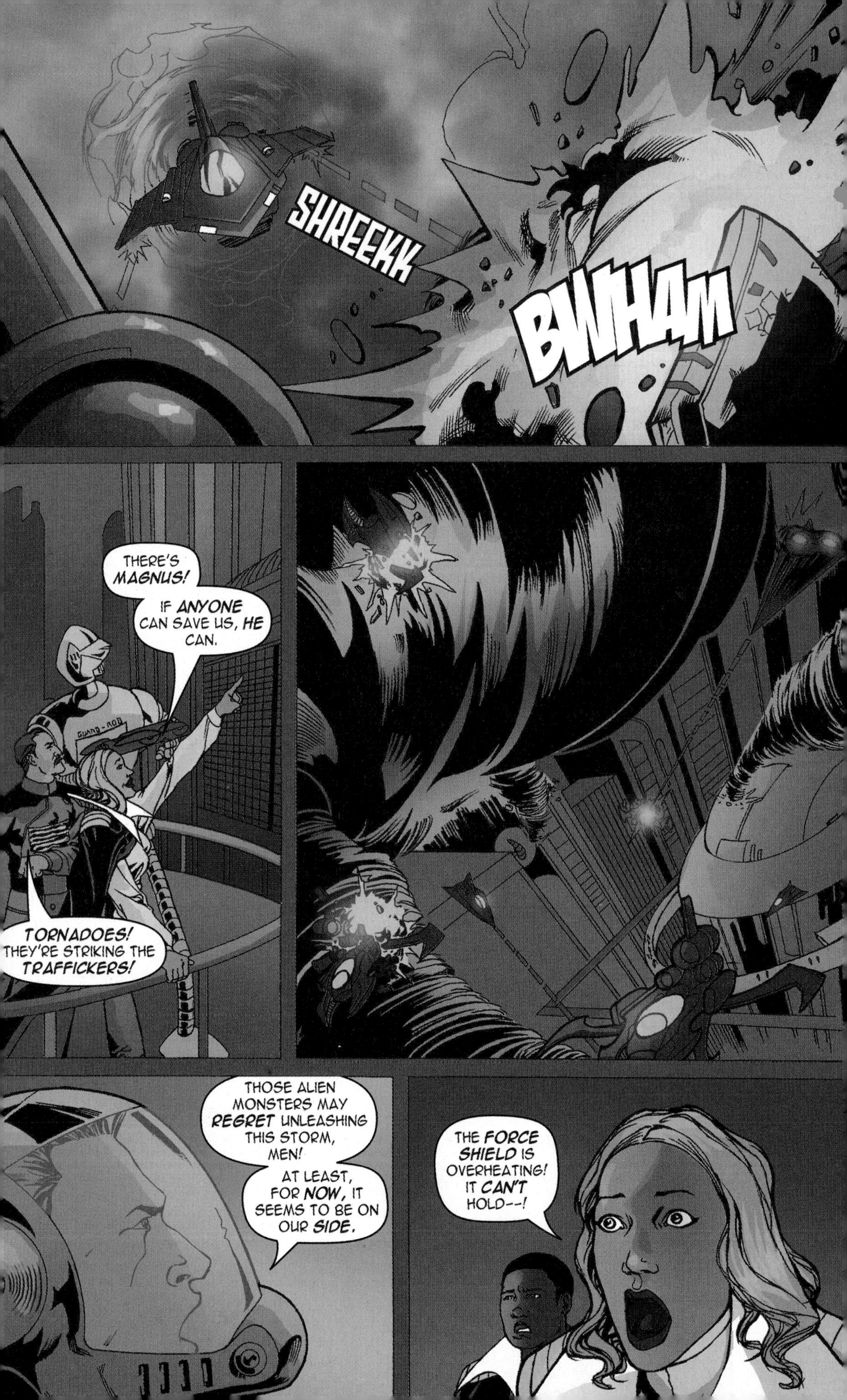
SHREEKK
BWHAM
THERE'S MAGNUS!
IF ANYONE CAN SAVE US, HE CAN.
TORNADOES! THEY'RE STRIKING THE TRAFFICKERS!
THOSE ALIEN MONSTERS MAY REGRET UNLEASHING THIS STORM, MEN!
AT LEAST, FOR NOW, IT SEEMS TO BE ON OUR SIDE.
THE FORCE SHIELD IS OVERHEATING! IT CAN'T HOLD--!

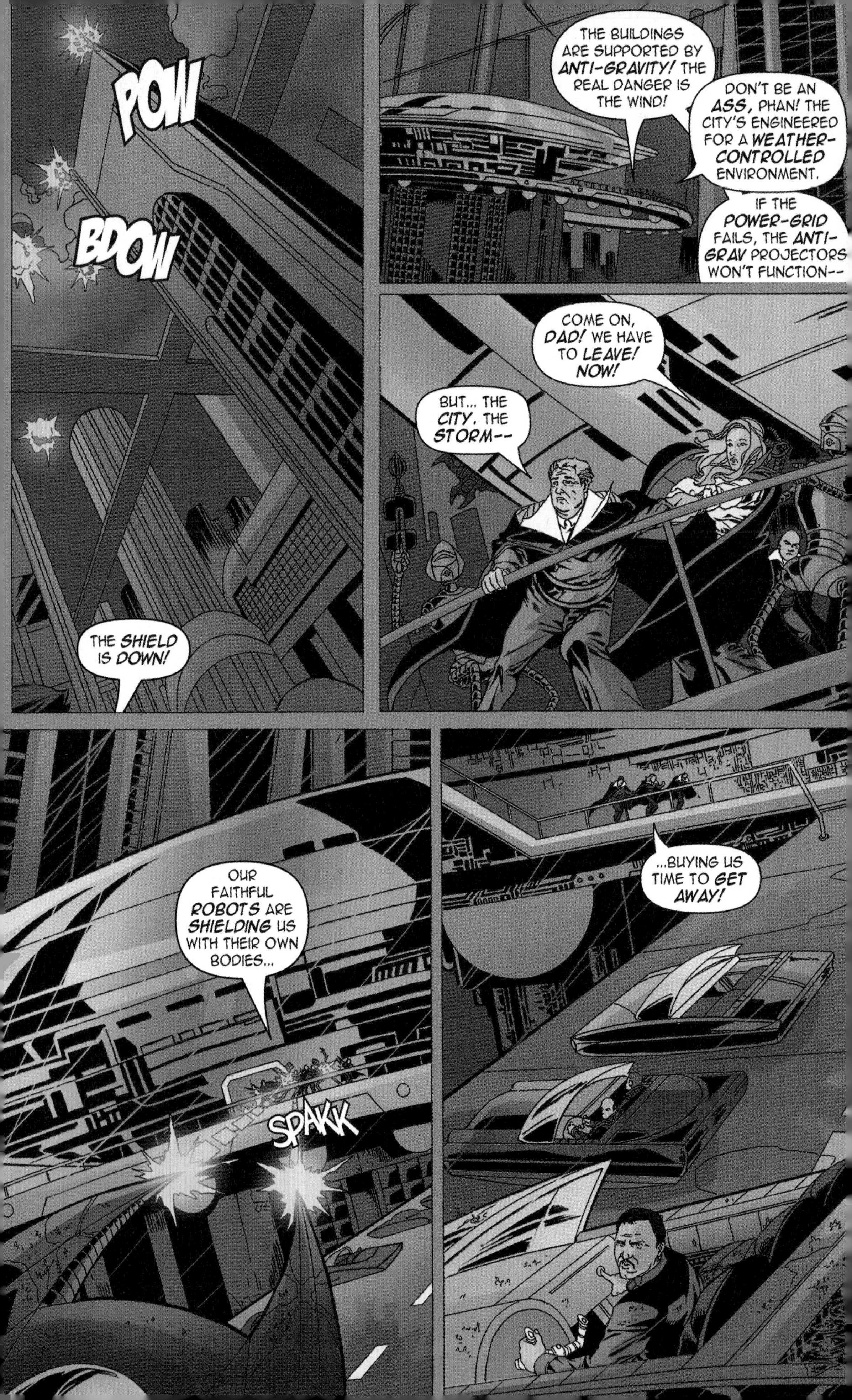
POW
BDOW
THE SHIELD IS DOWN!
THE BUILDINGS ARE SUPPORTED BY ANTI-GRAVITY! THE REAL DANGER IS THE WIND!
DON'T BE AN ASS, PHAN! THE CITY'S ENGINEERED FOR A WEATHER-CONTROLLED ENVIRONMENT.
IF THE POWER-GRID FAILS, THE ANTI-GRAV PROJECTORS WON'T FUNCTION--
COME ON, DAD! WE HAVE TO LEAVE! NOW!
BUT... THE CITY. THE STORM--
OUR FAITHFUL ROBOTS ARE SHIELDING US WITH THEIR OWN BODIES...
SPAKK
...BUYING US TIME TO GET AWAY!

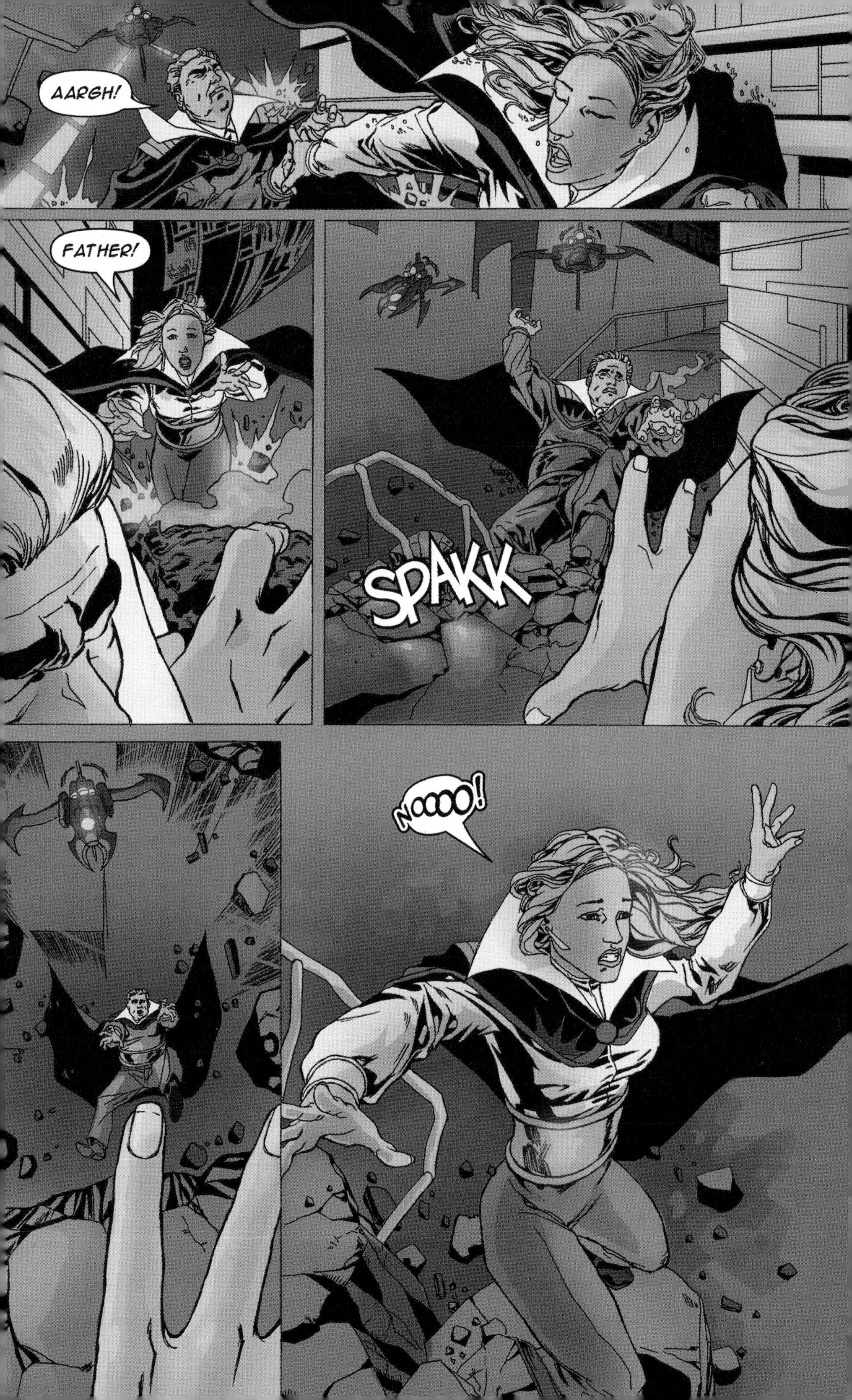
AARGH!
FATHER!
SPAKK
NOOOO!

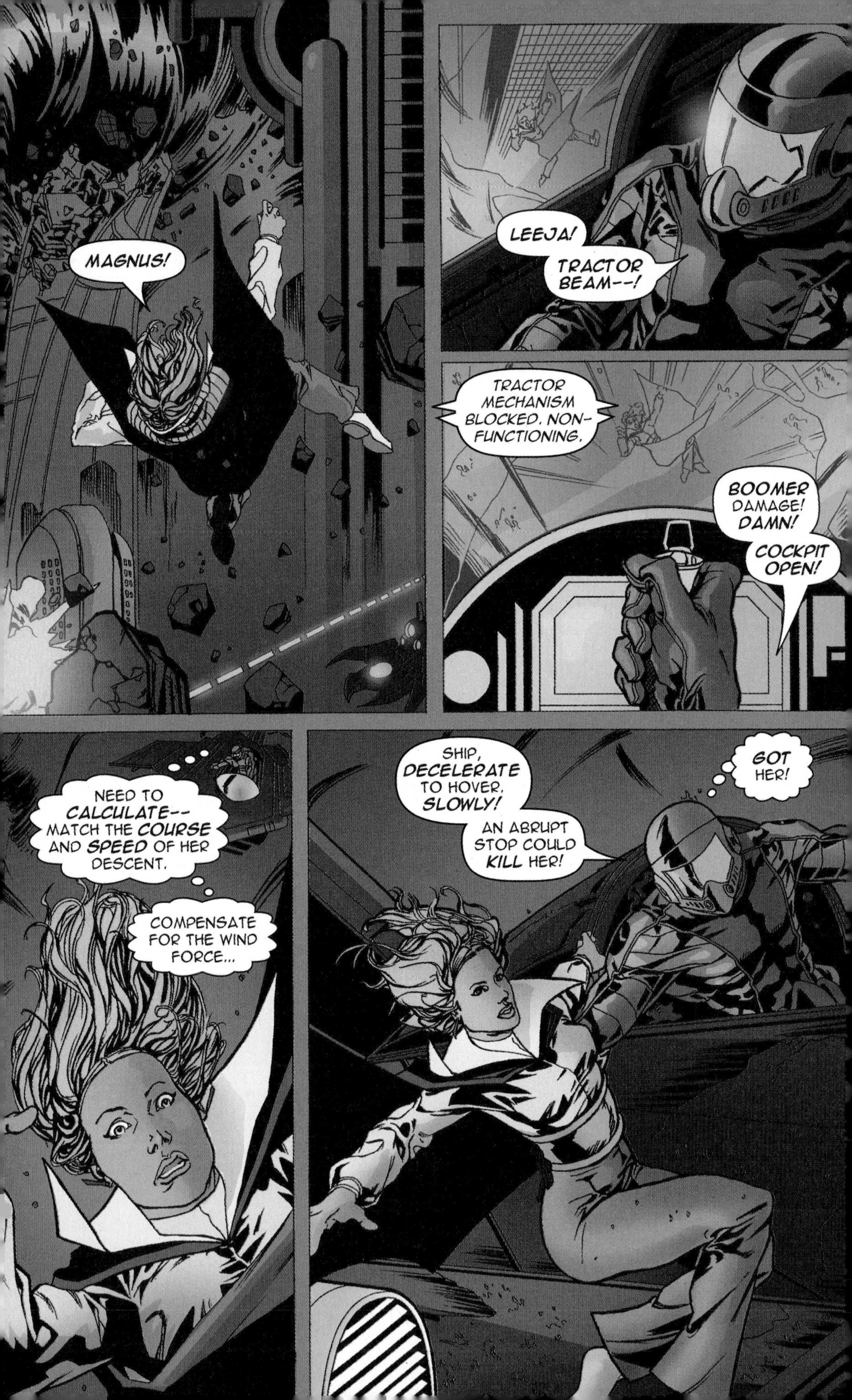
MAGNUS!
LEEJA!
TRACTOR BEAM--!
TRACTOR MECHANISM BLOCKED. NON-FUNCTIONING.
BOOMER DAMAGE! DAMN!
COCKPIT OPEN!
NEED TO CALCULATE-- MATCH THE COURSE AND SPEED OF HER DESCENT.
COMPENSATE FOR THE WIND FORCE...
SHIP, DECELERATE TO HOVER. SLOWLY!
AN ABRUPT STOP COULD KILL HER!
GOT HER!

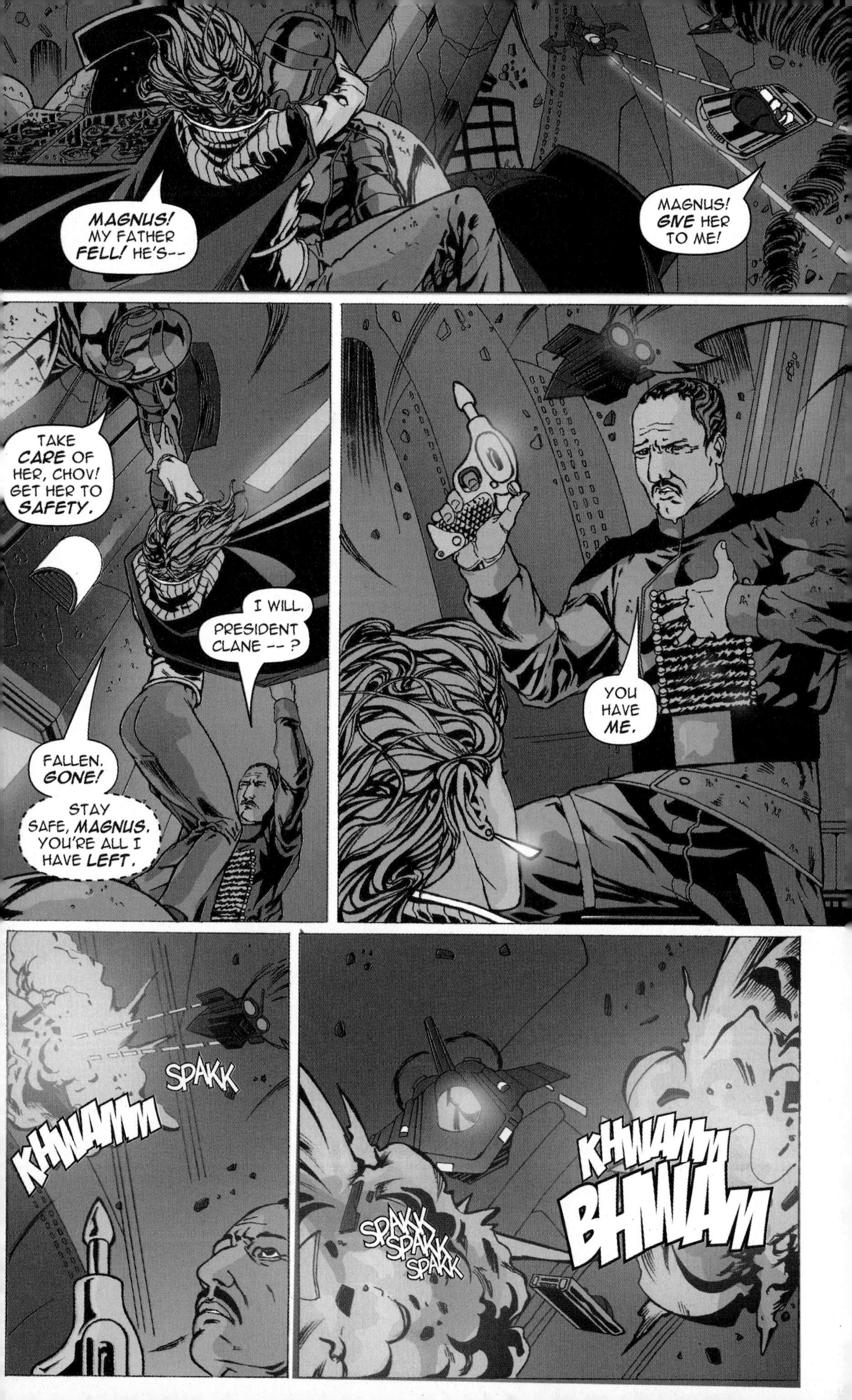
MAGNUS! MY FATHER FELL! HE'S--
MAGNUS! GIVE HER TO ME!
TAKE CARE OF HER, CHOV! GET HER TO SAFETY.
I WILL, PRESIDENT CLANE -- ?
FALLEN. GONE!
STAY SAFE, MAGNUS. YOU'RE ALL I HAVE LEFT.
YOU HAVE ME.
SPAKK
KHWAMM
KHWAMM
BHWAM
SPAKK SPAKK SPAKK

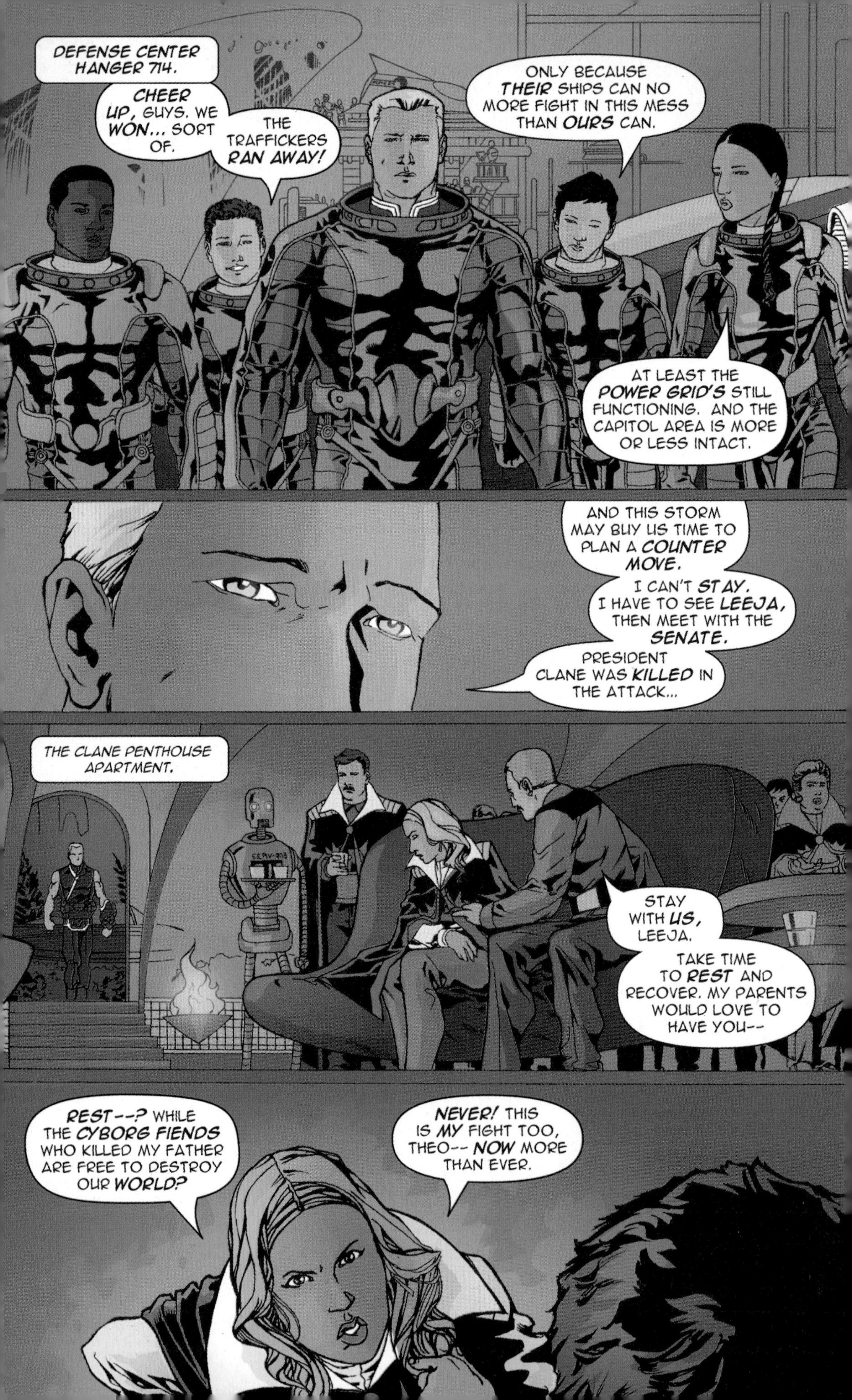
DEFENSE CENTER HANGER 714.
CHEER UP, GUYS. WE WON... SORT OF.
THE TRAFFICKERS RAN AWAY!
ONLY BECAUSE THEIR SHIPS CAN NO MORE FIGHT IN THIS MESS THAN OURS CAN.
AT LEAST THE POWER GRID'S STILL FUNCTIONING. AND THE CAPITOL AREA IS MORE OR LESS INTACT.
AND THIS STORM MAY BUY US TIME TO PLAN A COUNTER MOVE.
I CAN'T STAY. I HAVE TO SEE LEEJA, THEN MEET WITH THE SENATE.
PRESIDENT CLANE WAS KILLED IN THE ATTACK...
THE CLANE PENTHOUSE APARTMENT.
SERV-213
STAY WITH US, LEEJA.
TAKE TIME TO REST AND RECOVER. MY PARENTS WOULD LOVE TO HAVE YOU--
REST--? WHILE THE CYBORG FIENDS WHO KILLED MY FATHER ARE FREE TO DESTROY OUR WORLD?
NEVER! THIS IS MY FIGHT TOO, THEO-- NOW MORE THAN EVER.

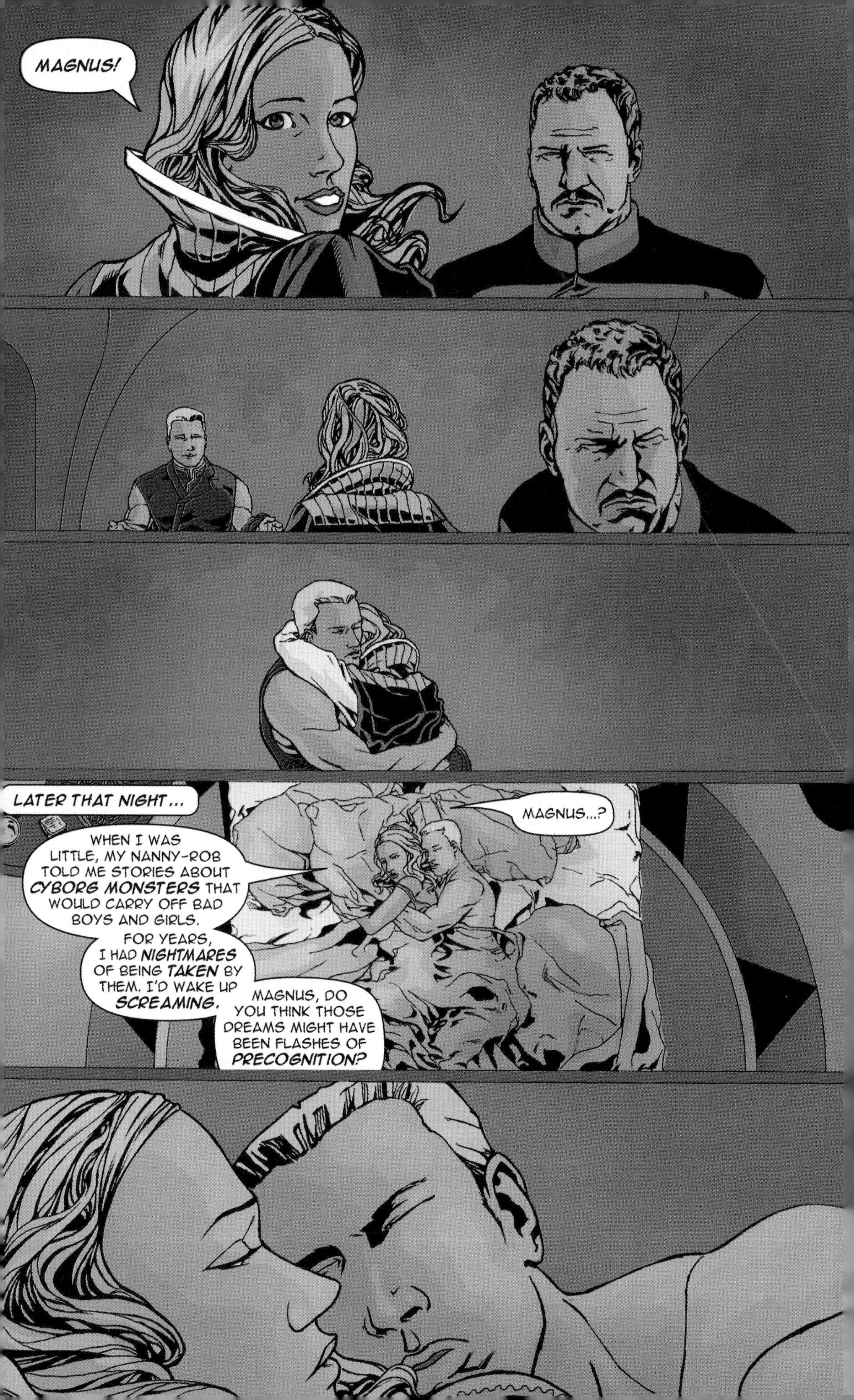
MAGNUS!
LATER THAT NIGHT...
MAGNUS...?
WHEN I WAS LITTLE, MY NANNY-ROB TOLD ME STORIES ABOUT CYBORG MONSTERS THAT WOULD CARRY OFF BAD BOYS AND GIRLS.
FOR YEARS, I HAD NIGHTMARES OF BEING TAKEN BY THEM. I'D WAKE UP SCREAMING.
MAGNUS, DO YOU THINK THOSE DREAMS MIGHT HAVE BEEN FLASHES OF PRECOGNITION?

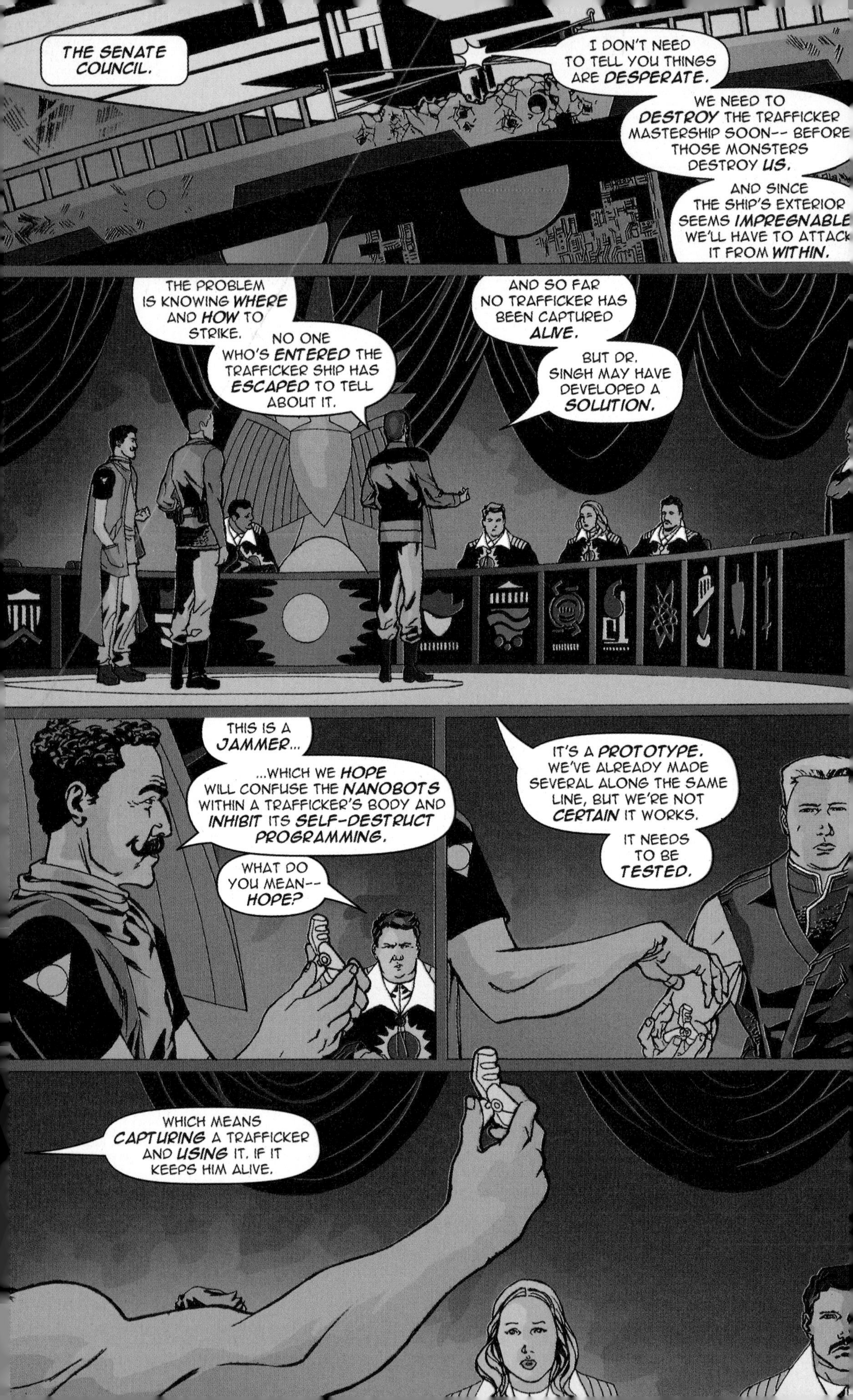
THE SENATE COUNCIL.
I DON'T NEED TO TELL YOU THINGS ARE DESPERATE.
WE NEED TO DESTROY THE TRAFFICKER MASTERSHIP SOON-- BEFORE THOSE MONSTERS DESTROY US.
AND SINCE THE SHIP'S EXTERIOR SEEMS IMPREGNABLE WE'LL HAVE TO ATTACK IT FROM WITHIN.
THE PROBLEM IS KNOWING WHERE AND HOW TO STRIKE.
NO ONE WHO'S ENTERED THE TRAFFICKER SHIP HAS ESCAPED TO TELL ABOUT IT.
AND SO FAR NO TRAFFICKER HAS BEEN CAPTURED ALIVE.
BUT DR. SINGH MAY HAVE DEVELOPED A SOLUTION.
THIS IS A JAMMER...
...WHICH WE HOPE WILL CONFUSE THE NANOBOTS WITHIN A TRAFFICKER'S BODY AND INHIBIT ITS SELF-DESTRUCT PROGRAMMING.
WHAT DO YOU MEAN-- HOPE?
IT'S A PROTOTYPE. WE'VE ALREADY MADE SEVERAL ALONG THE SAME LINE, BUT WE'RE NOT CERTAIN IT WORKS.
IT NEEDS TO BE TESTED.
WHICH MEANS CAPTURING A TRAFFICKER AND USING IT. IF IT KEEPS HIM ALIVE.

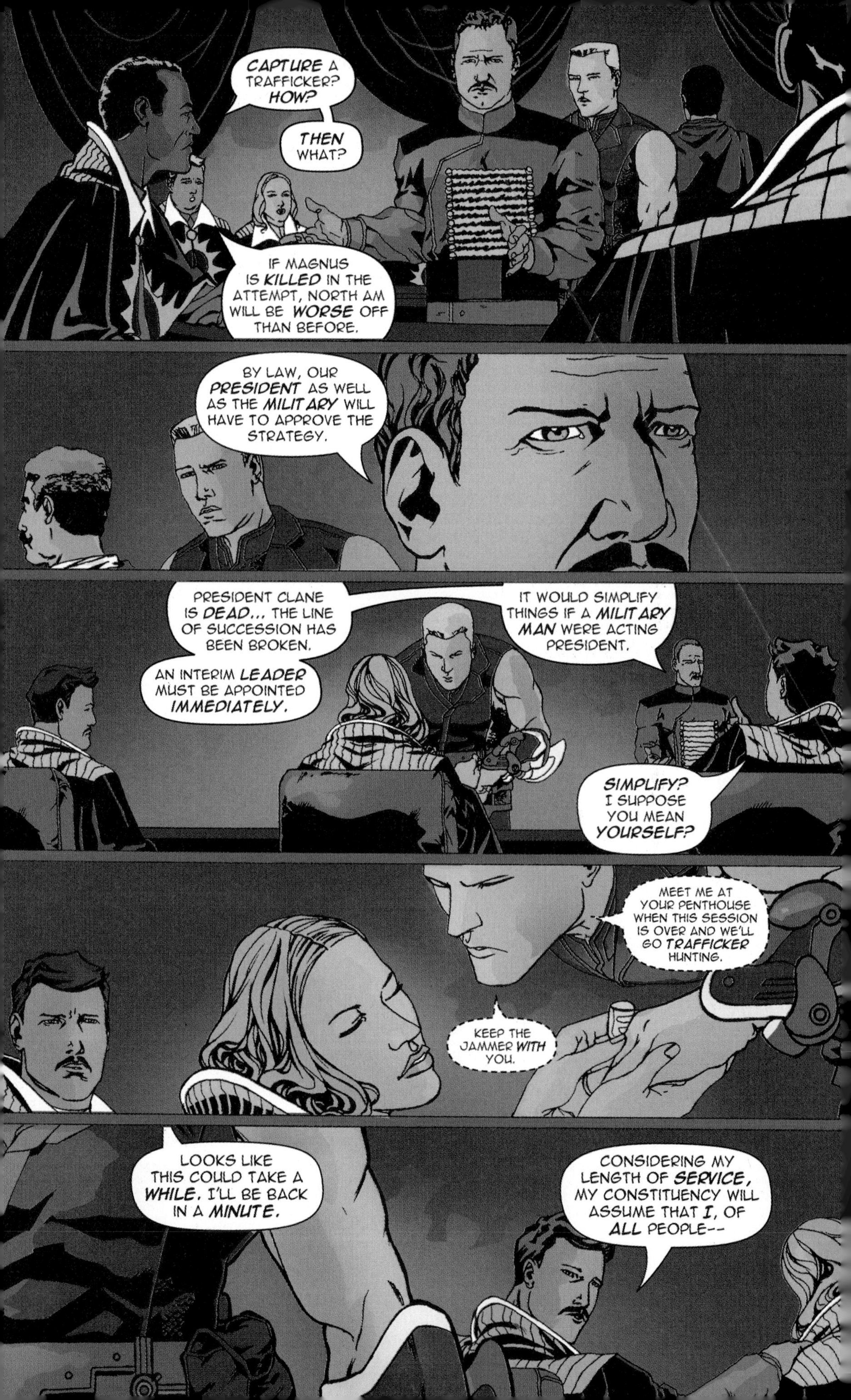
CAPTURE A TRAFFICKER? HOW?
THEN WHAT?
IF MAGNUS IS KILLED IN THE ATTEMPT, NORTH AM WILL BE WORSE OFF THAN BEFORE.
BY LAW, OUR PRESIDENT AS WELL AS THE MILITARY WILL HAVE TO APPROVE THE STRATEGY.
PRESIDENT CLANE IS DEAD... THE LINE OF SUCCESSION HAS BEEN BROKEN.
AN INTERIM LEADER MUST BE APPOINTED IMMEDIATELY.
IT WOULD SIMPLIFY THINGS IF A MILITARY MAN WERE ACTING PRESIDENT.
SIMPLIFY? I SUPPOSE YOU MEAN YOURSELF?
MEET ME AT YOUR PENTHOUSE WHEN THIS SESSION IS OVER AND WE'LL GO TRAFFICKER HUNTING.
KEEP THE JAMMER WITH YOU.
LOOKS LIKE THIS COULD TAKE A WHILE. I'LL BE BACK IN A MINUTE.
CONSIDERING MY LENGTH OF SERVICE, MY CONSTITUENCY WILL ASSUME THAT I, OF ALL PEOPLE--

BRIDGE. TRAFFICKER MASTERSHIP.

<<I HAVE BEEN INFORMED THAT THE FLESHWARE HAVE INVENTED A DEVICE TO *INHIBIT* OUR *SELF-LIQUIDATION* PROCESS.>>

<<IT IS PRESENTLY IN THE HANDS OF MAGNUS'S FEMALE, *LEEJA CLANE.*>>

<<A TRACER HAS BEEN PLACED ON HER. FOLLOW HER. *BRING* ME THE *DEVICE*... AND THE *FEMALE.*>>

<<HER CAPTURE WILL *DISTRACT* MAGNUS & SIMPLIFY OUR CONQUE OF *EARTH.*>>

THE CLANE PENTHOUSE.

<<WHAT A *DISASTER!* BY THE TIME WE WIN THIS PLANET, THERE'LL BE NOTHING LEFT.>>

<<NOT *YOUR* CONCERN! JUST GET THE *FEMALE!*>>

TRAFFICKERS! DANGER!

INTRUDERS!

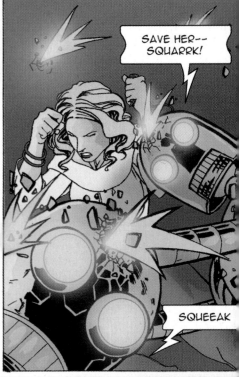

SAVE HER-- SQUARRK!

SQUEEAK

CYBORGS! *NO!*

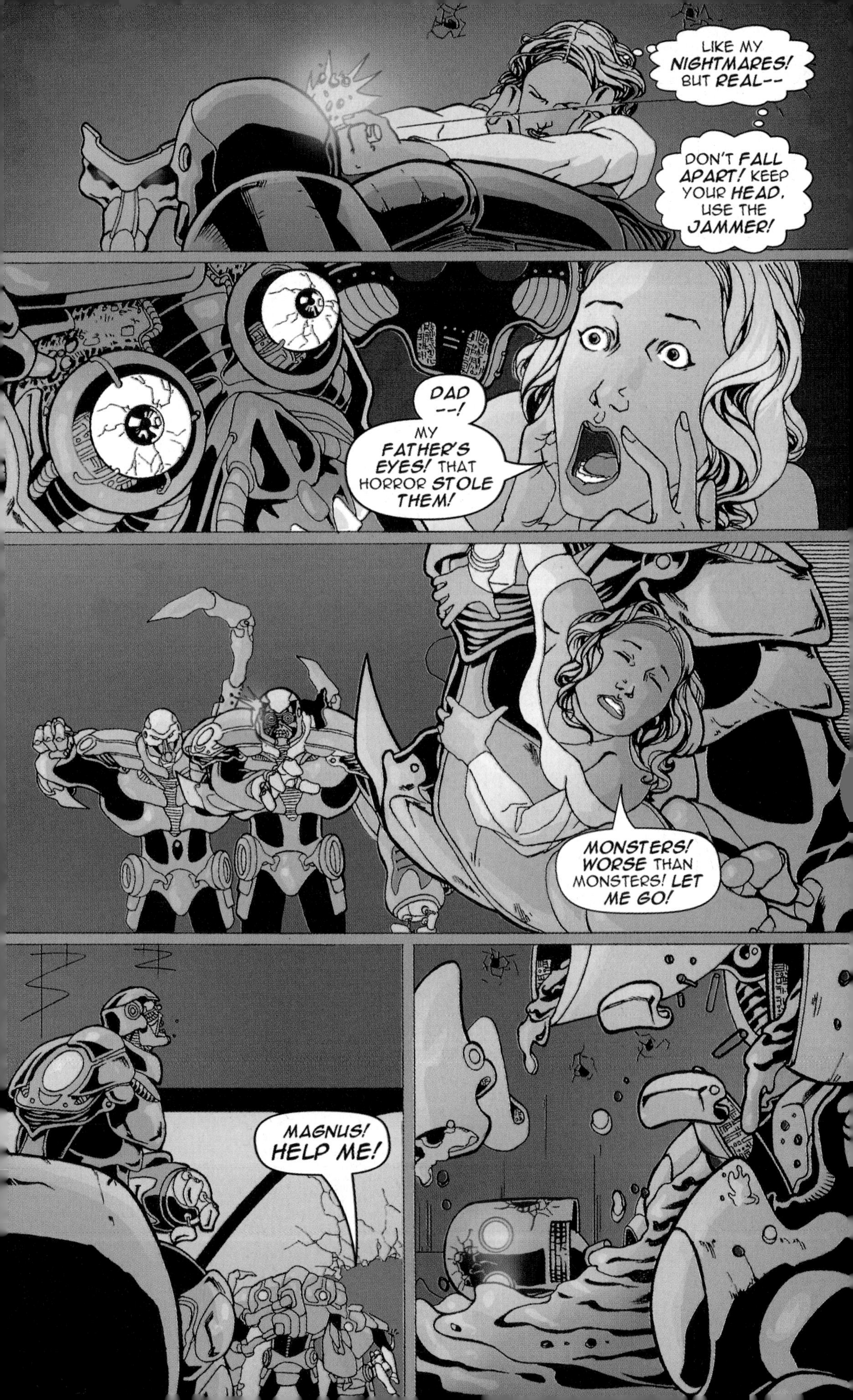
LIKE MY NIGHTMARES! BUT REAL--
DON'T FALL APART! KEEP YOUR HEAD. USE THE JAMMER!
DAD --!
MY FATHER'S EYES! THAT HORROR STOLE THEM!
MONSTERS! WORSE THAN MONSTERS! LET ME GO!
MAGNUS! HELP ME!

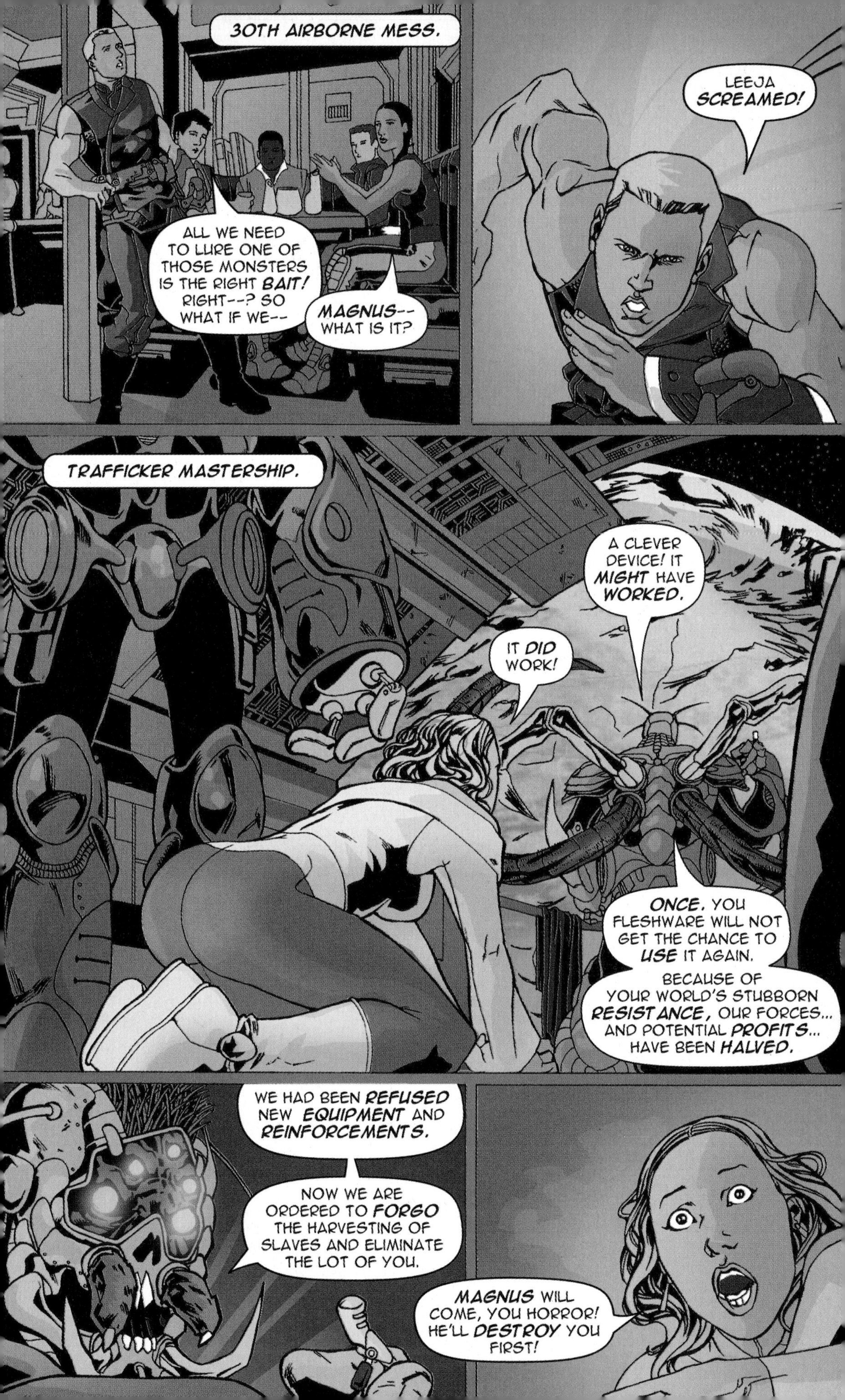
30TH AIRBORNE MESS.
ALL WE NEED TO LURE ONE OF THOSE MONSTERS IS THE RIGHT BAIT! RIGHT--? SO WHAT IF WE--
MAGNUS-- WHAT IS IT?
LEEJA SCREAMED!
TRAFFICKER MASTERSHIP.
A CLEVER DEVICE! IT MIGHT HAVE WORKED.
IT DID WORK!
ONCE. YOU FLESHWARE WILL NOT GET THE CHANCE TO USE IT AGAIN.
BECAUSE OF YOUR WORLD'S STUBBORN RESISTANCE, OUR FORCES... AND POTENTIAL PROFITS... HAVE BEEN HALVED.
WE HAD BEEN REFUSED NEW EQUIPMENT AND REINFORCEMENTS.
NOW WE ARE ORDERED TO FORGO THE HARVESTING OF SLAVES AND ELIMINATE THE LOT OF YOU.
MAGNUS WILL COME, YOU HORROR! HE'LL DESTROY YOU FIRST!

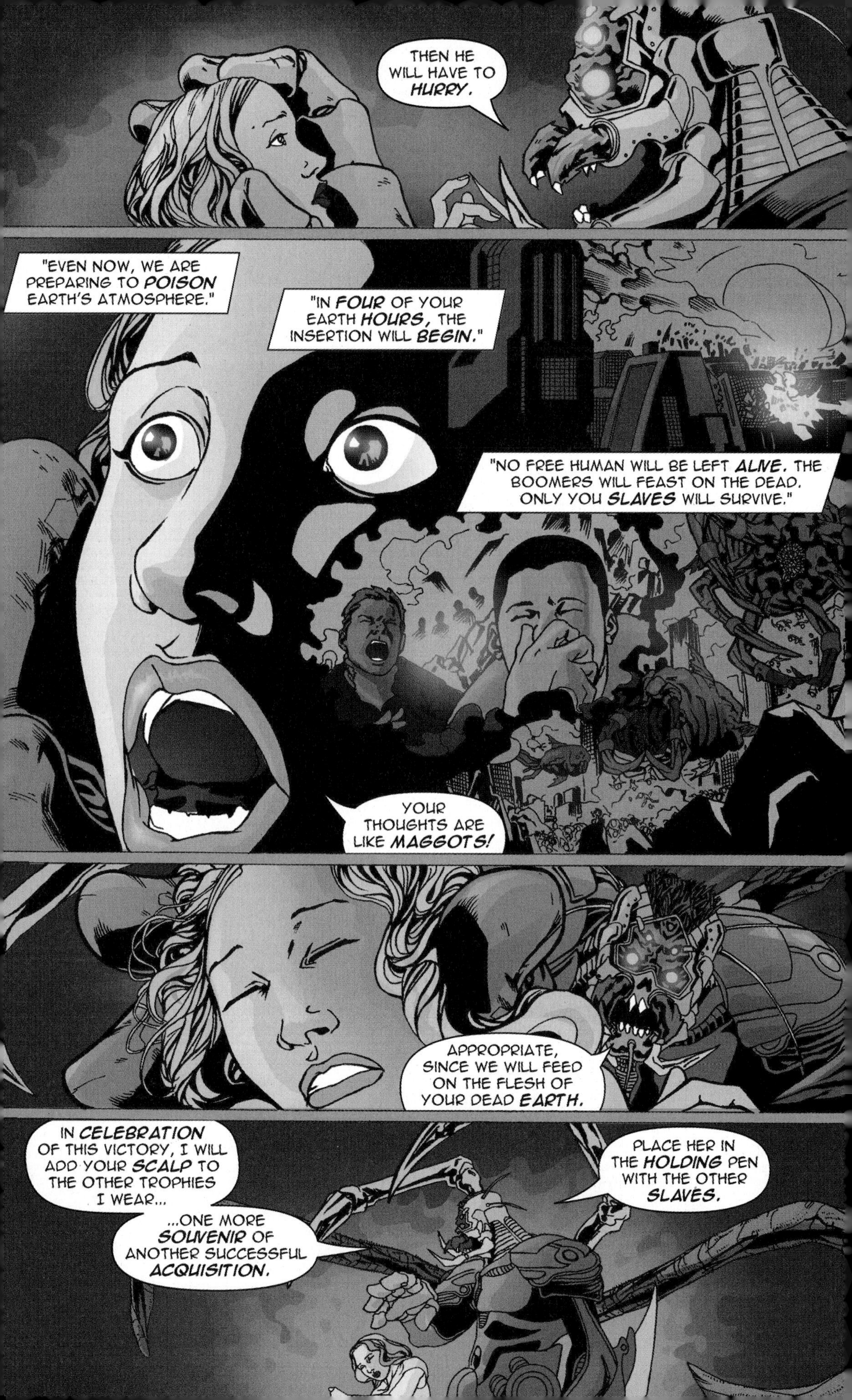
THEN HE WILL HAVE TO HURRY.
"EVEN NOW, WE ARE PREPARING TO POISON EARTH'S ATMOSPHERE."
"IN FOUR OF YOUR EARTH HOURS, THE INSERTION WILL BEGIN."
"NO FREE HUMAN WILL BE LEFT ALIVE. THE BOOMERS WILL FEAST ON THE DEAD. ONLY YOU SLAVES WILL SURVIVE."
YOUR THOUGHTS ARE LIKE MAGGOTS!
APPROPRIATE, SINCE WE WILL FEED ON THE FLESH OF YOUR DEAD EARTH.
IN CELEBRATION OF THIS VICTORY, I WILL ADD YOUR SCALP TO THE OTHER TROPHIES I WEAR...
...ONE MORE SOUVENIR OF ANOTHER SUCCESSFUL ACQUISITION.
PLACE HER IN THE HOLDING PEN WITH THE OTHER SLAVES.

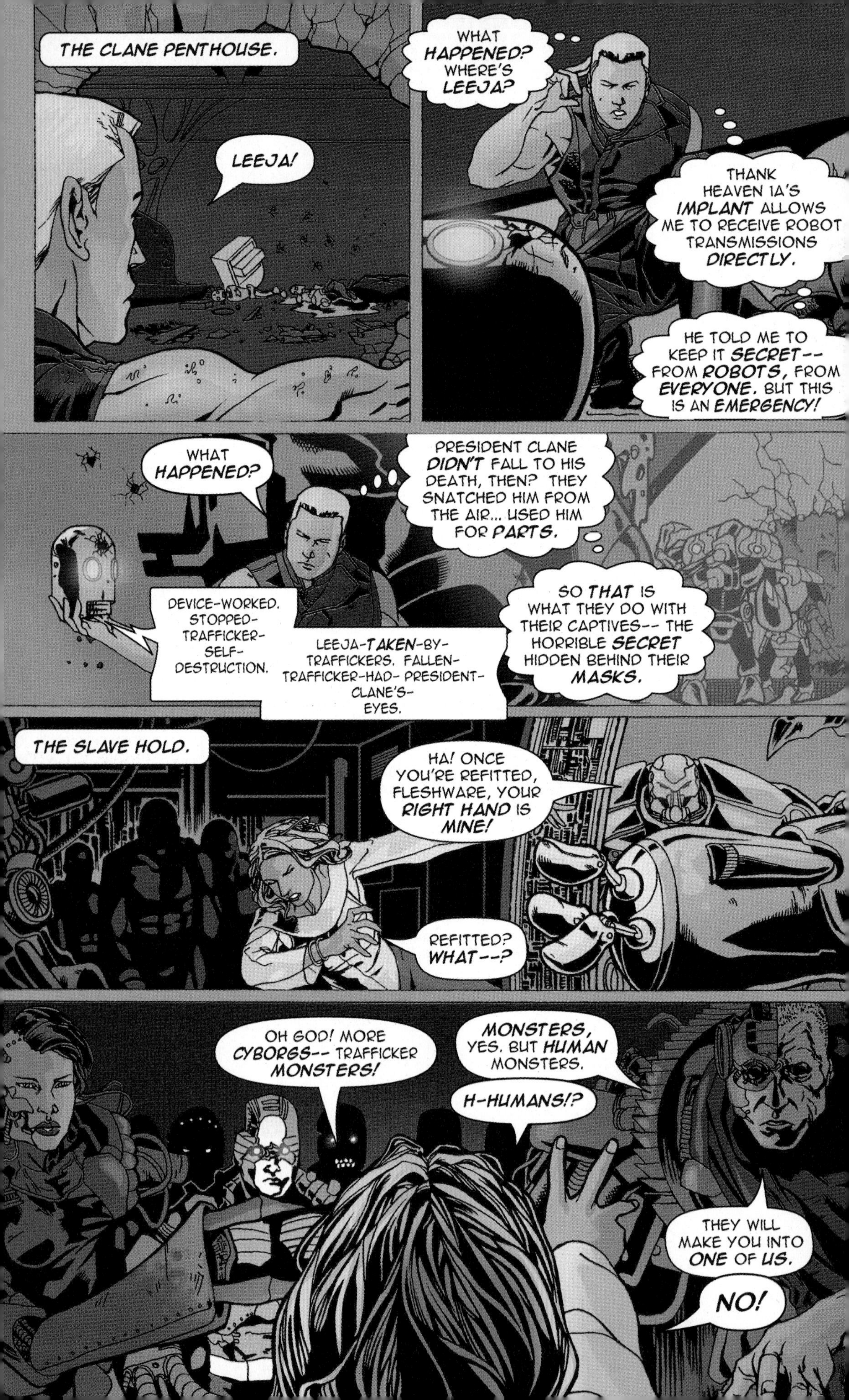
THE CLANE PENTHOUSE.
LEEJA!
WHAT HAPPENED? WHERE'S LEEJA?
THANK HEAVEN IA'S IMPLANT ALLOWS ME TO RECEIVE ROBOT TRANSMISSIONS DIRECTLY.
HE TOLD ME TO KEEP IT SECRET-- FROM ROBOTS, FROM EVERYONE. BUT THIS IS AN EMERGENCY!
WHAT HAPPENED?
PRESIDENT CLANE DIDN'T FALL TO HIS DEATH, THEN? THEY SNATCHED HIM FROM THE AIR... USED HIM FOR PARTS.
DEVICE-WORKED. STOPPED-TRAFFICKER-SELF-DESTRUCTION.
LEEJA-TAKEN-BY-TRAFFICKERS. FALLEN-TRAFFICKER-HAD- PRESIDENT-CLANE'S-EYES.
SO THAT IS WHAT THEY DO WITH THEIR CAPTIVES-- THE HORRIBLE SECRET HIDDEN BEHIND THEIR MASKS.
THE SLAVE HOLD.
HA! ONCE YOU'RE REFITTED, FLESHWARE, YOUR RIGHT HAND IS MINE!
REFITTED? WHAT--?
OH GOD! MORE CYBORGS-- TRAFFICKER MONSTERS!
MONSTERS, YES. BUT HUMAN MONSTERS.
H-HUMANS!?
THEY WILL MAKE YOU INTO ONE OF US.
NO!

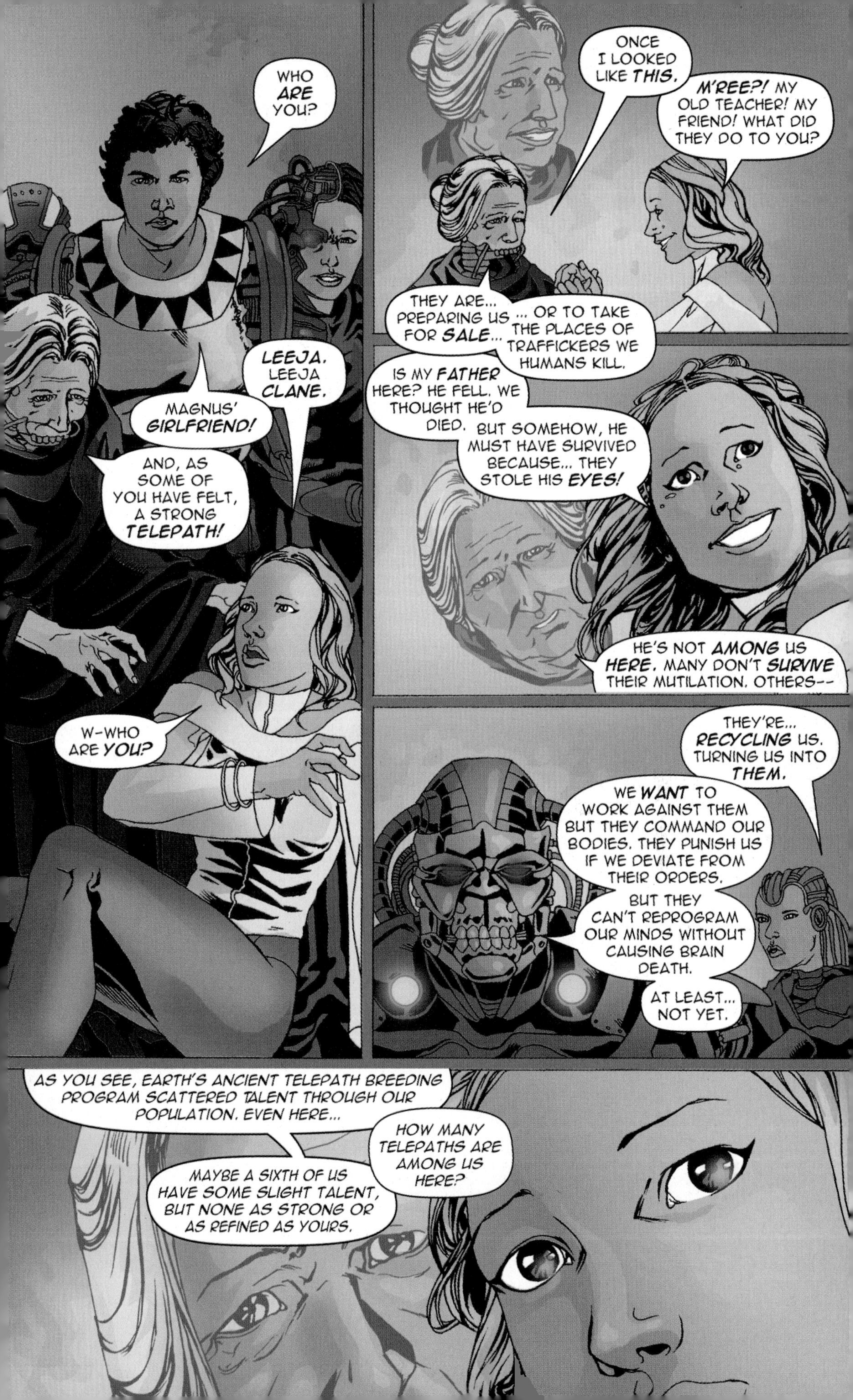
WHO ARE YOU?
LEEJA. LEEJA CLANE.
MAGNUS' GIRLFRIEND!
AND, AS SOME OF YOU HAVE FELT, A STRONG TELEPATH!
W-WHO ARE YOU?
ONCE I LOOKED LIKE THIS.
M'REE?! MY OLD TEACHER! MY FRIEND! WHAT DID THEY DO TO YOU?
THEY ARE... PREPARING US FOR SALE...
... OR TO TAKE THE PLACES OF TRAFFICKERS WE HUMANS KILL.
IS MY FATHER HERE? HE FELL. WE THOUGHT HE'D DIED.
BUT SOMEHOW, HE MUST HAVE SURVIVED BECAUSE... THEY STOLE HIS EYES!
HE'S NOT AMONG US HERE. MANY DON'T SURVIVE THEIR MUTILATION. OTHERS--
THEY'RE... RECYCLING US. TURNING US INTO THEM.
WE WANT TO WORK AGAINST THEM BUT THEY COMMAND OUR BODIES. THEY PUNISH US IF WE DEVIATE FROM THEIR ORDERS.
BUT THEY CAN'T REPROGRAM OUR MINDS WITHOUT CAUSING BRAIN DEATH.
AT LEAST... NOT YET.
AS YOU SEE, EARTH'S ANCIENT TELEPATH BREEDING PROGRAM SCATTERED TALENT THROUGH OUR POPULATION. EVEN HERE...
HOW MANY TELEPATHS ARE AMONG US HERE?
MAYBE A SIXTH OF US HAVE SOME SLIGHT TALENT, BUT NONE AS STRONG OR AS REFINED AS YOURS.

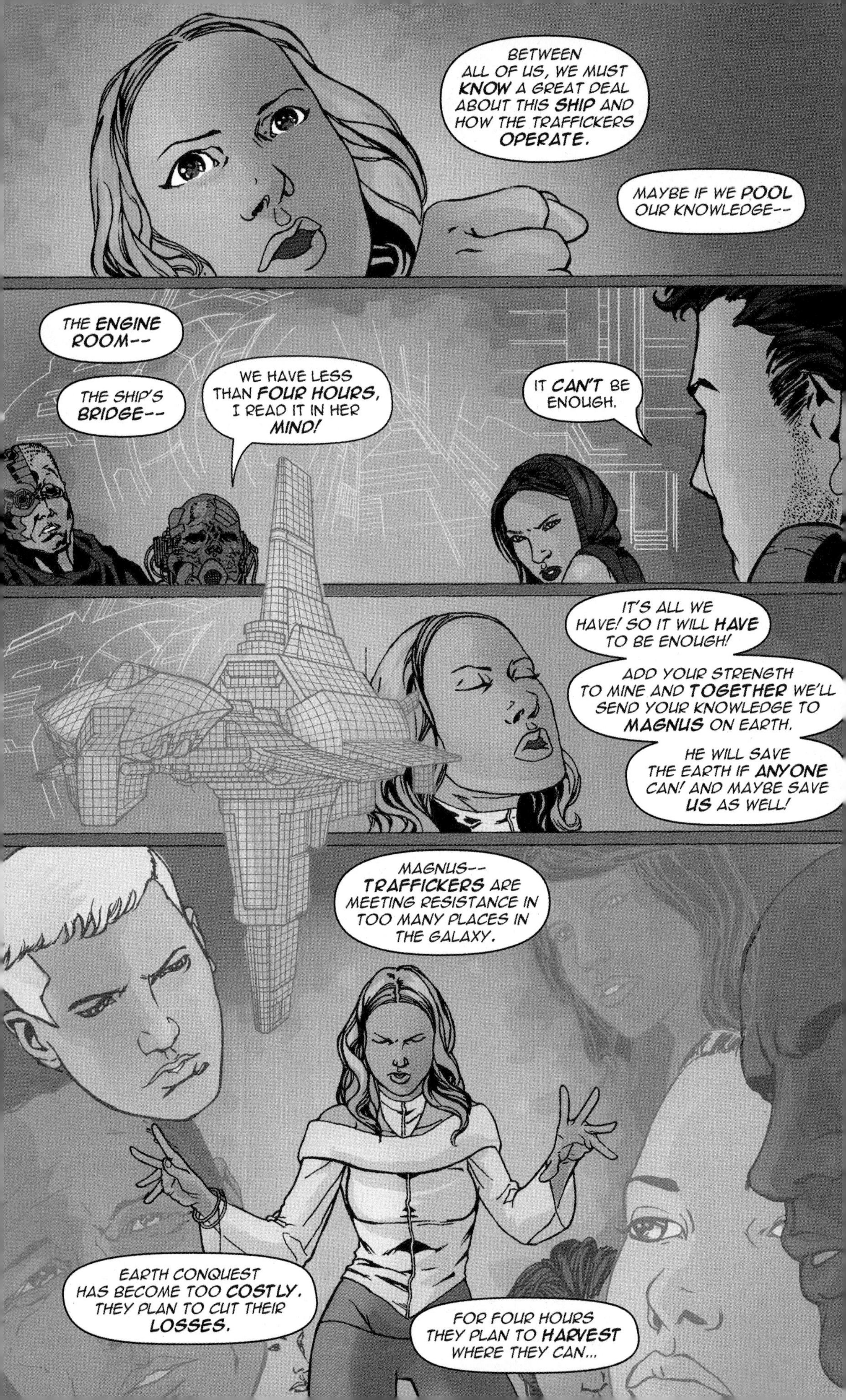
BETWEEN ALL OF US, WE MUST KNOW A GREAT DEAL ABOUT THIS SHIP AND HOW THE TRAFFICKERS OPERATE.
MAYBE IF WE POOL OUR KNOWLEDGE--
THE ENGINE ROOM--
THE SHIP'S BRIDGE--
WE HAVE LESS THAN FOUR HOURS, I READ IT IN HER MIND!
IT CAN'T BE ENOUGH.
IT'S ALL WE HAVE! SO IT WILL HAVE TO BE ENOUGH!
ADD YOUR STRENGTH TO MINE AND TOGETHER WE'LL SEND YOUR KNOWLEDGE TO MAGNUS ON EARTH.
HE WILL SAVE THE EARTH IF ANYONE CAN! AND MAYBE SAVE US AS WELL!
MAGNUS-- TRAFFICKERS ARE MEETING RESISTANCE IN TOO MANY PLACES IN THE GALAXY.
EARTH CONQUEST HAS BECOME TOO COSTLY. THEY PLAN TO CUT THEIR LOSSES.
FOR FOUR HOURS THEY PLAN TO HARVEST WHERE THEY CAN...

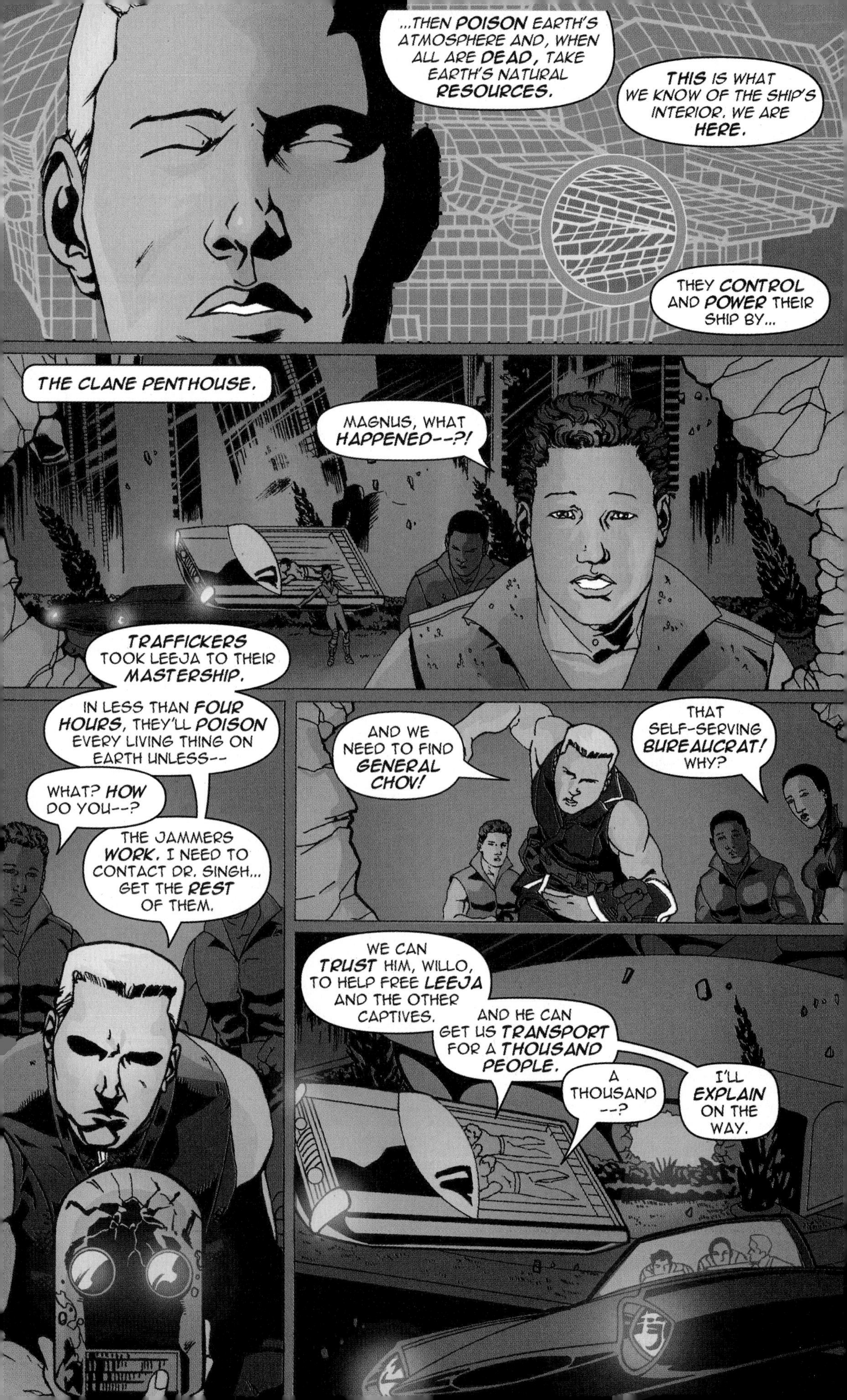
...THEN POISON EARTH'S ATMOSPHERE AND, WHEN ALL ARE DEAD, TAKE EARTH'S NATURAL RESOURCES.
THIS IS WHAT WE KNOW OF THE SHIP'S INTERIOR. WE ARE HERE.
THEY CONTROL AND POWER THEIR SHIP BY...
THE CLANE PENTHOUSE.
MAGNUS, WHAT HAPPENED--?!
TRAFFICKERS TOOK LEEJA TO THEIR MASTERSHIP.
IN LESS THAN FOUR HOURS, THEY'LL POISON EVERY LIVING THING ON EARTH UNLESS--
WHAT? HOW DO YOU--?
THE JAMMERS WORK. I NEED TO CONTACT DR. SINGH... GET THE REST OF THEM.
AND WE NEED TO FIND GENERAL CHOV!
THAT SELF-SERVING BUREAUCRAT! WHY?
WE CAN TRUST HIM, WILLO, TO HELP FREE LEEJA AND THE OTHER CAPTIVES.
AND HE CAN GET US TRANSPORT FOR A THOUSAND PEOPLE.
A THOUSAND --?
I'LL EXPLAIN ON THE WAY.

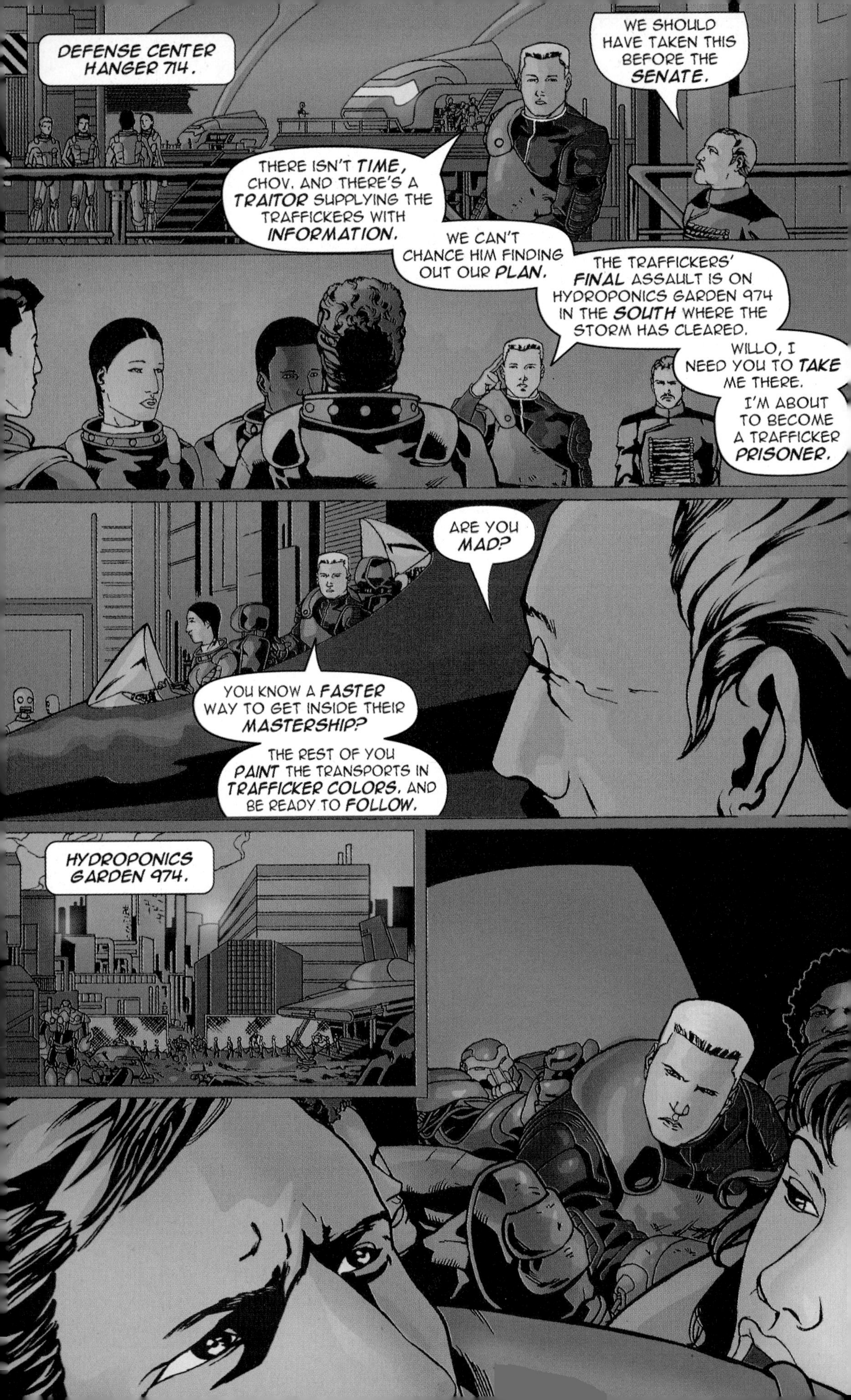
DEFENSE CENTER HANGER 714.
WE SHOULD HAVE TAKEN THIS BEFORE THE SENATE.
THERE ISN'T TIME, CHOV. AND THERE'S A TRAITOR SUPPLYING THE TRAFFICKERS WITH INFORMATION.
WE CAN'T CHANCE HIM FINDING OUT OUR PLAN.
THE TRAFFICKERS' FINAL ASSAULT IS ON HYDROPONICS GARDEN 974 IN THE SOUTH WHERE THE STORM HAS CLEARED.
WILLO, I NEED YOU TO TAKE ME THERE.
I'M ABOUT TO BECOME A TRAFFICKER PRISONER.
ARE YOU MAD?
YOU KNOW A FASTER WAY TO GET INSIDE THEIR MASTERSHIP?
THE REST OF YOU PAINT THE TRANSPORTS IN TRAFFICKER COLORS, AND BE READY TO FOLLOW.
HYDROPONICS GARDEN 974.

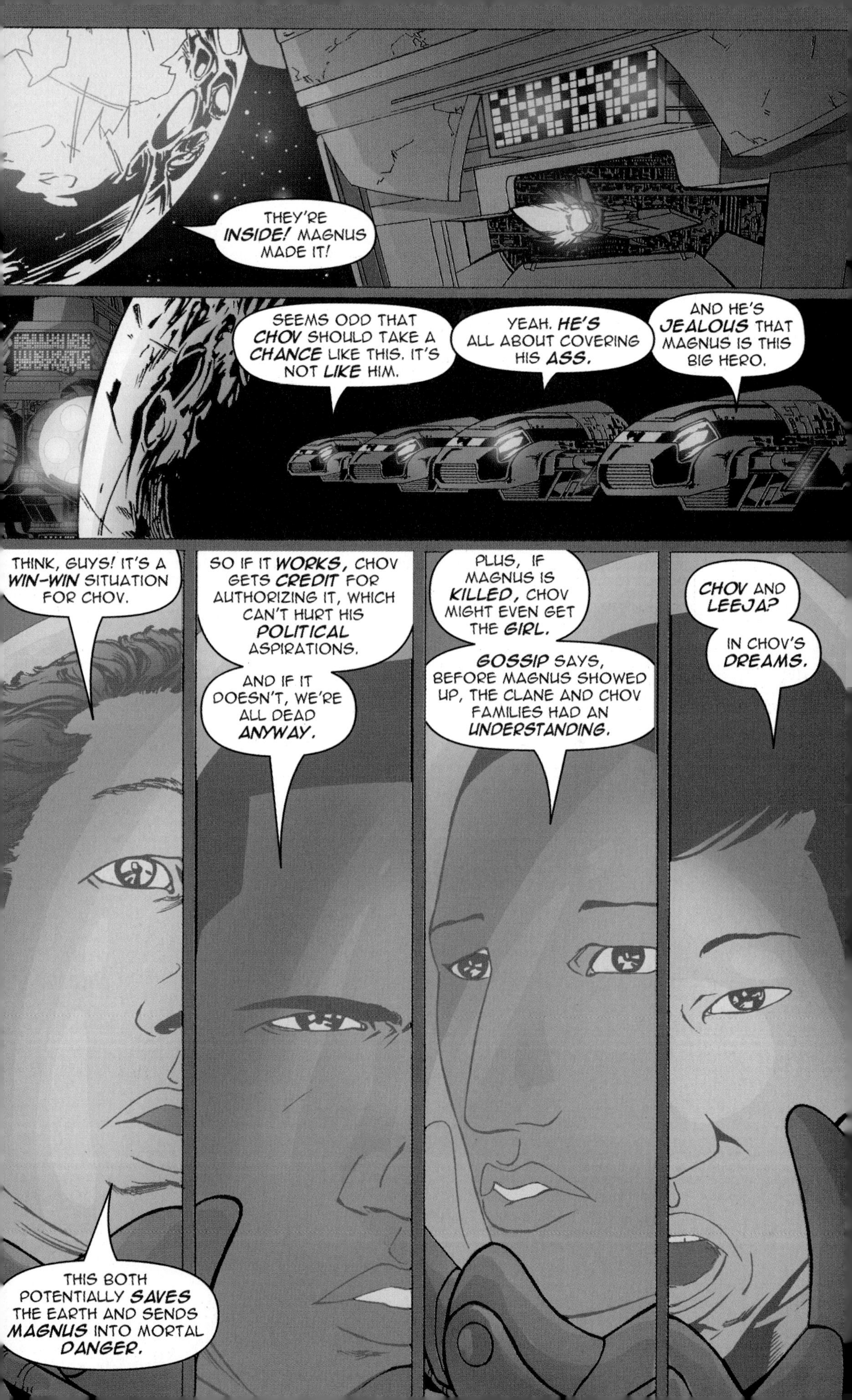

THEY'RE INSIDE! MAGNUS MADE IT!
SEEMS ODD THAT CHOV SHOULD TAKE A CHANCE LIKE THIS. IT'S NOT LIKE HIM.
YEAH. HE'S ALL ABOUT COVERING HIS ASS.
AND HE'S JEALOUS THAT MAGNUS IS THIS BIG HERO.
THINK, GUYS! IT'S A WIN-WIN SITUATION FOR CHOV.
THIS BOTH POTENTIALLY SAVES THE EARTH AND SENDS MAGNUS INTO MORTAL DANGER.
SO IF IT WORKS, CHOV GETS CREDIT FOR AUTHORIZING IT, WHICH CAN'T HURT HIS POLITICAL ASPIRATIONS.
AND IF IT DOESN'T, WE'RE ALL DEAD ANYWAY.
PLUS, IF MAGNUS IS KILLED, CHOV MIGHT EVEN GET THE GIRL.
GOSSIP SAYS, BEFORE MAGNUS SHOWED UP, THE CLANE AND CHOV FAMILIES HAD AN UNDERSTANDING.
CHOV AND LEEJA?
IN CHOV'S DREAMS.

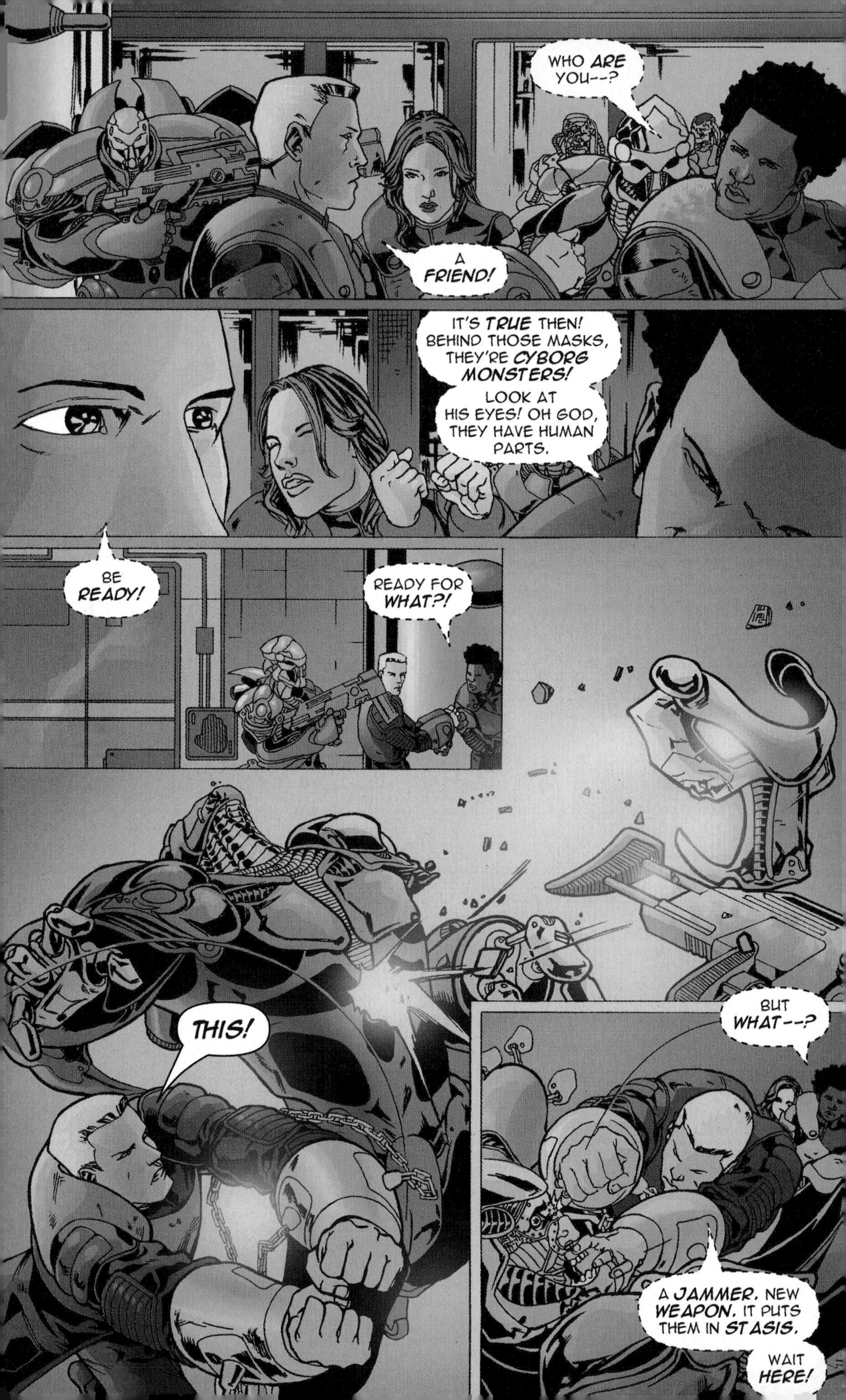
WHO ARE YOU--?
A FRIEND!
IT'S TRUE THEN! BEHIND THOSE MASKS, THEY'RE CYBORG MONSTERS!
LOOK AT HIS EYES! OH GOD, THEY HAVE HUMAN PARTS.
BE READY!
READY FOR WHAT?!
THIS!
BUT WHAT--?
A JAMMER. NEW WEAPON. IT PUTS THEM IN STASIS.
WAIT HERE!

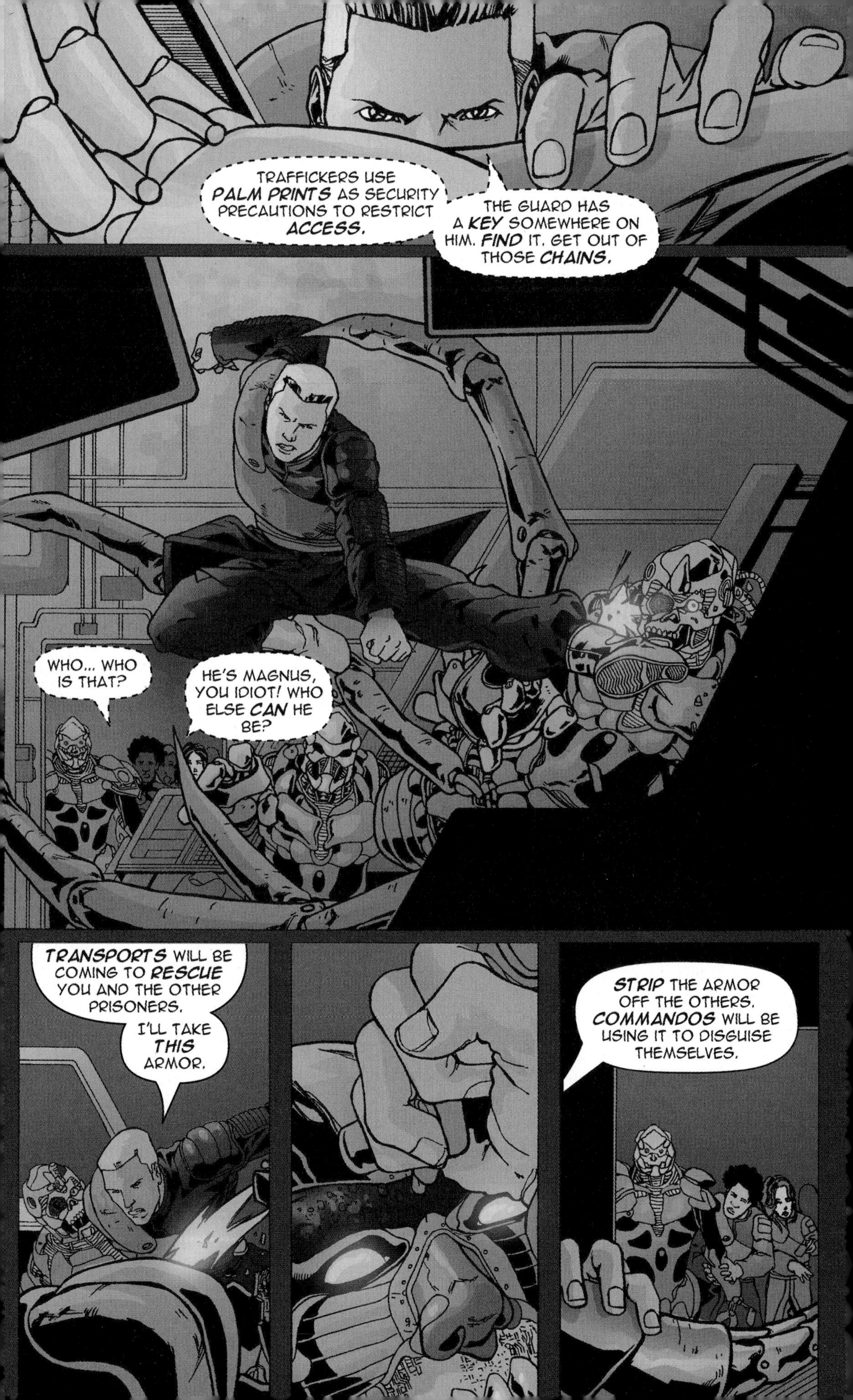
TRAFFICKERS USE PALM PRINTS AS SECURITY PRECAUTIONS TO RESTRICT ACCESS.
THE GUARD HAS A KEY SOMEWHERE ON HIM. FIND IT. GET OUT OF THOSE CHAINS.
WHO... WHO IS THAT?
HE'S MAGNUS, YOU IDIOT! WHO ELSE CAN HE BE?
TRANSPORTS WILL BE COMING TO RESCUE YOU AND THE OTHER PRISONERS.
I'LL TAKE THIS ARMOR.
STRIP THE ARMOR OFF THE OTHERS. COMMANDOS WILL BE USING IT TO DISGUISE THEMSELVES.

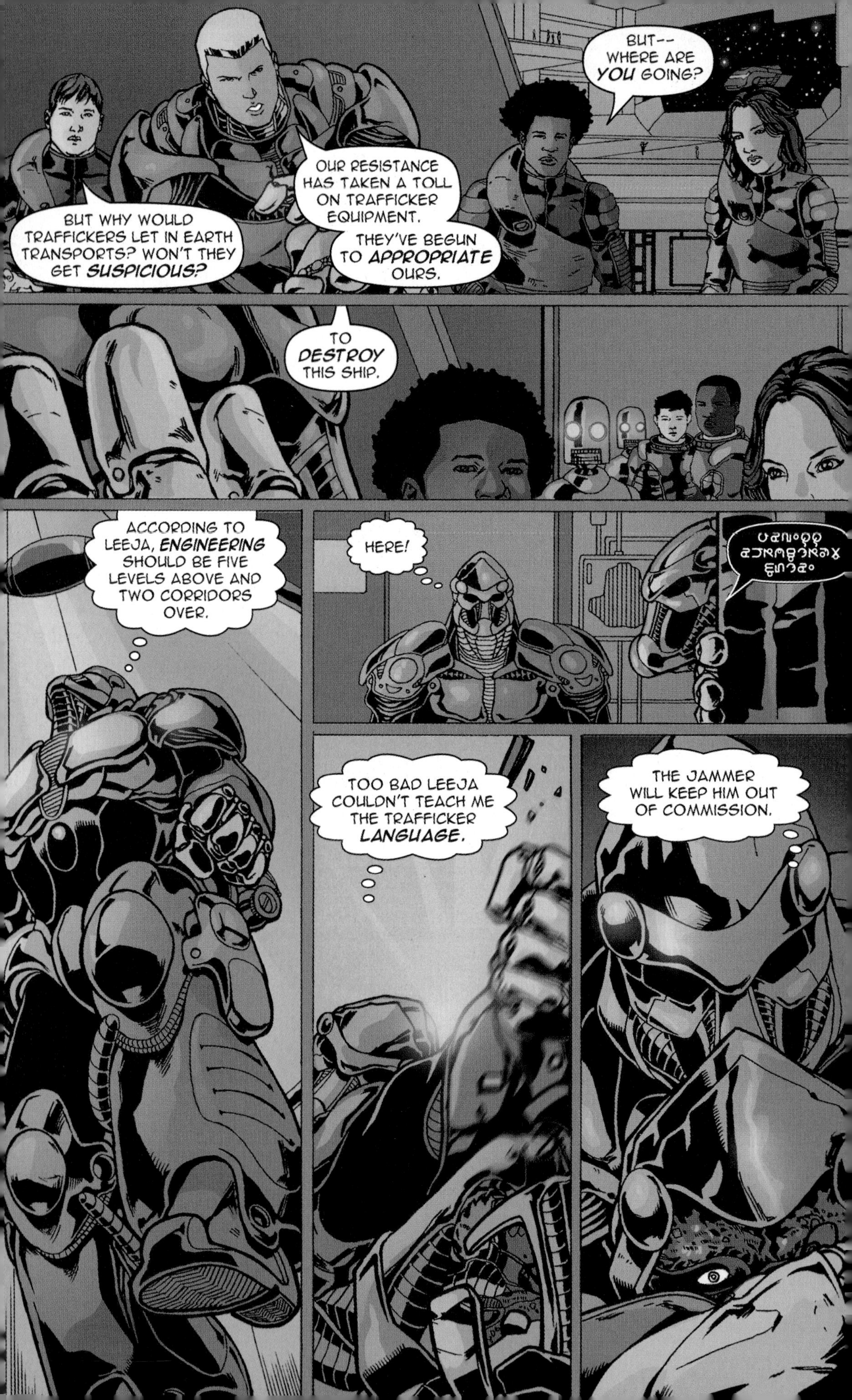
BUT-- WHERE ARE YOU GOING?
BUT WHY WOULD TRAFFICKERS LET IN EARTH TRANSPORTS? WON'T THEY GET SUSPICIOUS?
OUR RESISTANCE HAS TAKEN A TOLL ON TRAFFICKER EQUIPMENT.
THEY'VE BEGUN TO APPROPRIATE OURS.
TO DESTROY THIS SHIP.
ACCORDING TO LEEJA, ENGINEERING SHOULD BE FIVE LEVELS ABOVE AND TWO CORRIDORS OVER.
HERE!
TOO BAD LEEJA COULDN'T TEACH ME THE TRAFFICKER LANGUAGE.
THE JAMMER WILL KEEP HIM OUT OF COMMISSION.

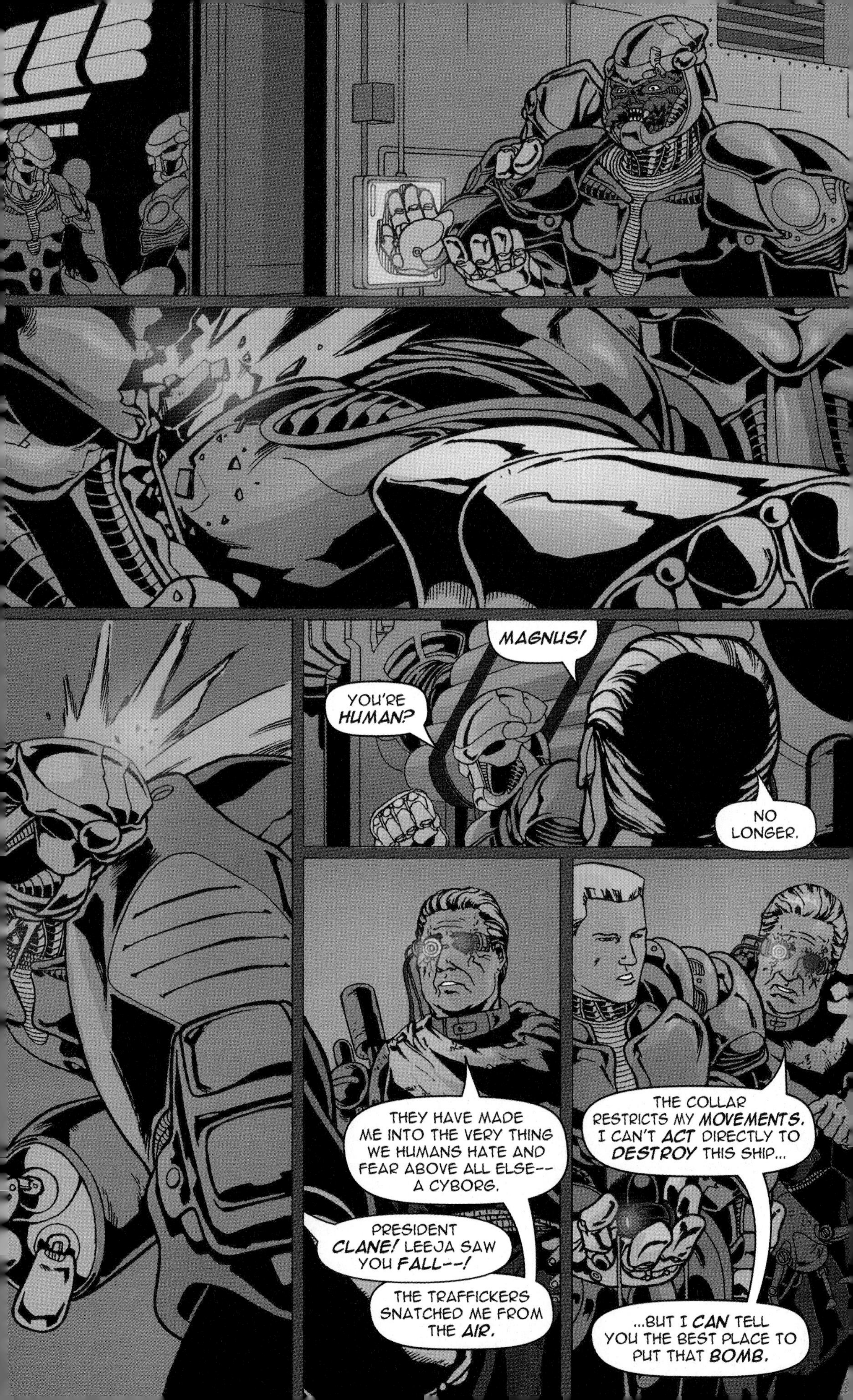
MAGNUS!
YOU'RE HUMAN?
NO LONGER.
THEY HAVE MADE ME INTO THE VERY THING WE HUMANS HATE AND FEAR ABOVE ALL ELSE-- A CYBORG.
PRESIDENT CLANE! LEEJA SAW YOU FALL--!
THE TRAFFICKERS SNATCHED ME FROM THE AIR.
THE COLLAR RESTRICTS MY MOVEMENTS. I CAN'T ACT DIRECTLY TO DESTROY THIS SHIP...
...BUT I CAN TELL YOU THE BEST PLACE TO PUT THAT BOMB.

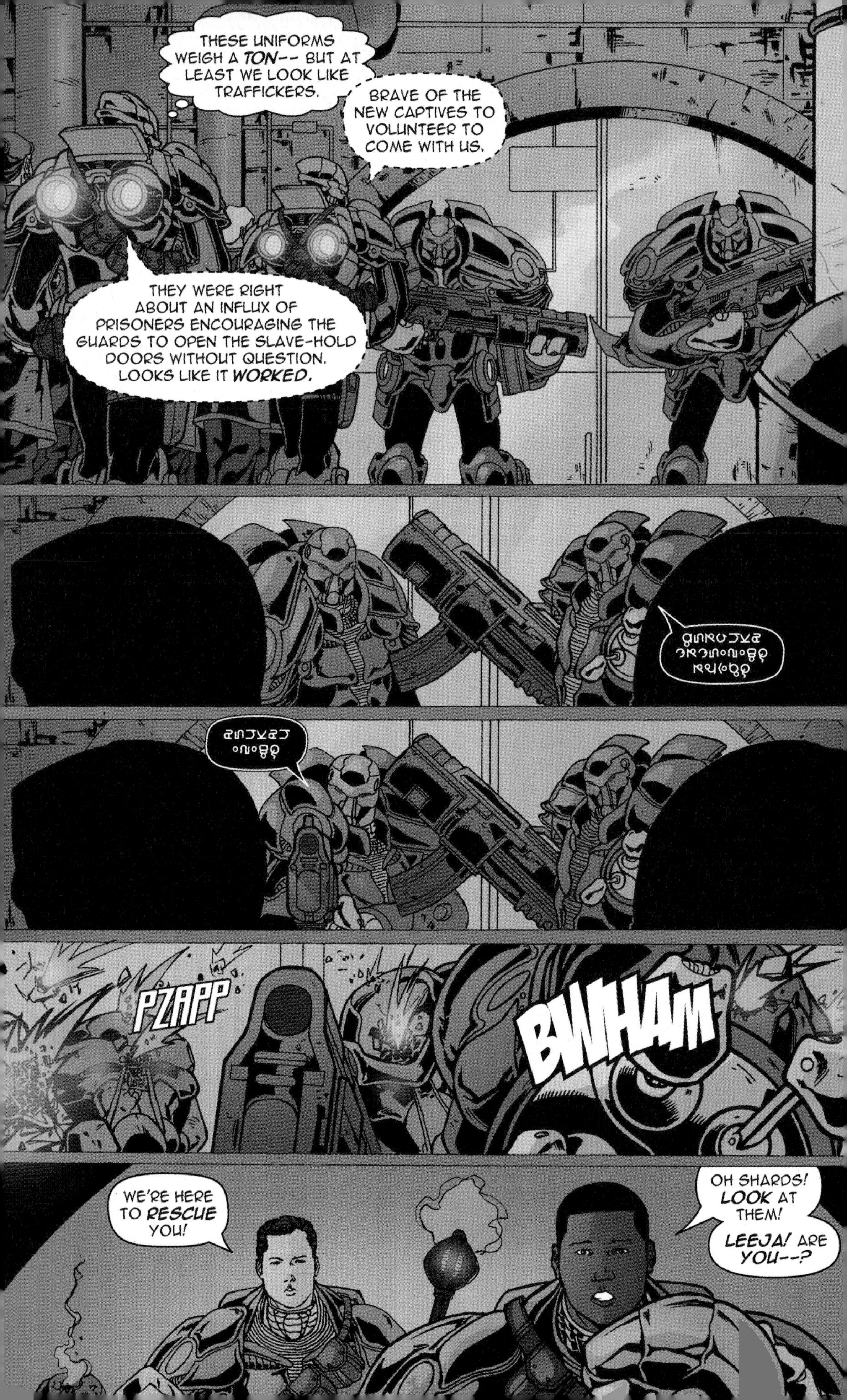
THESE UNIFORMS WEIGH A TON-- BUT AT LEAST WE LOOK LIKE TRAFFICKERS.
BRAVE OF THE NEW CAPTIVES TO VOLUNTEER TO COME WITH US.
THEY WERE RIGHT ABOUT AN INFLUX OF PRISONERS ENCOURAGING THE GUARDS TO OPEN THE SLAVE-HOLD DOORS WITHOUT QUESTION. LOOKS LIKE IT WORKED.
PZAPP
BWHAM
WE'RE HERE TO RESCUE YOU!
OH SHARDS! LOOK AT THEM!
LEEJA! ARE YOU--?

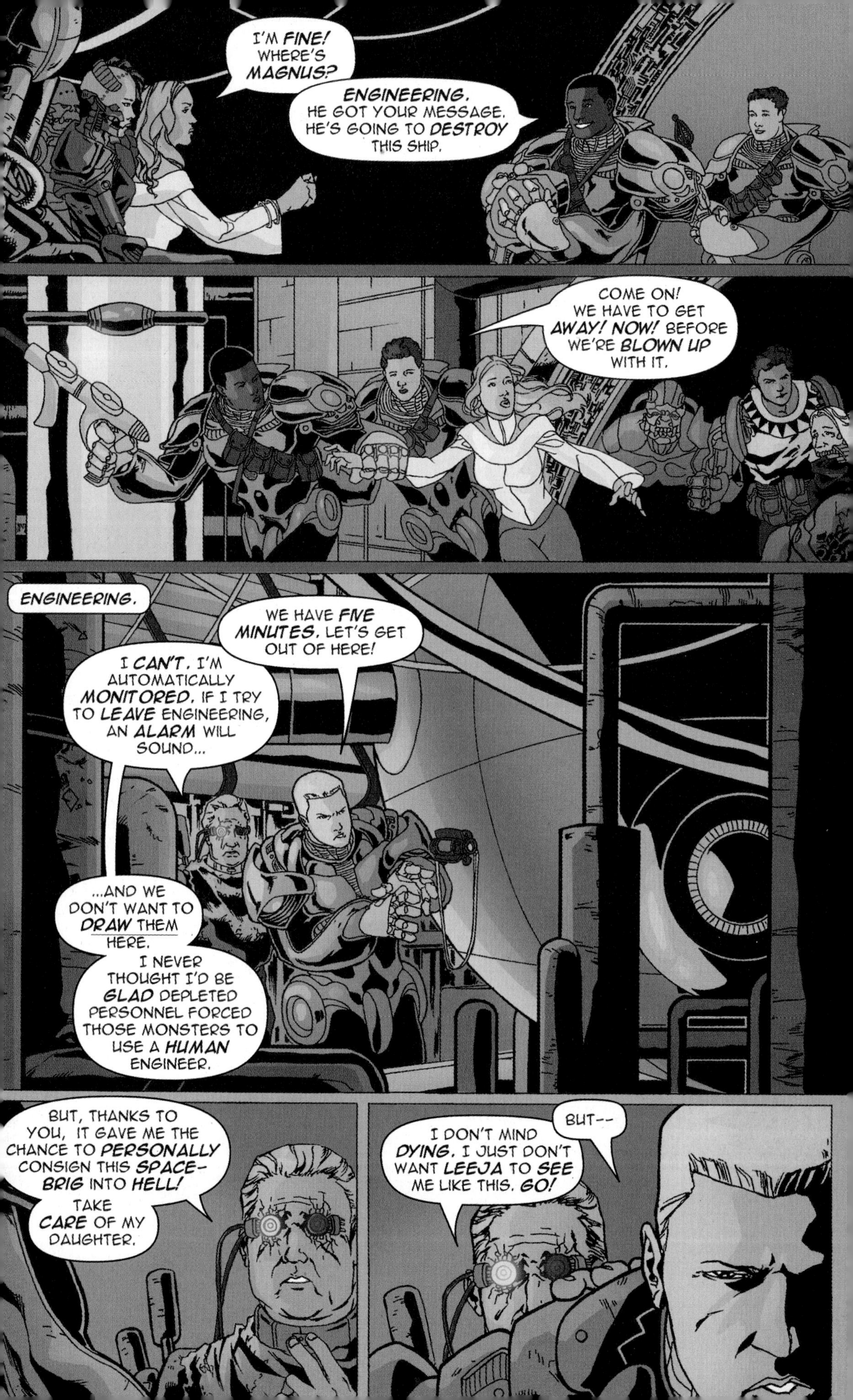
I'M FINE! WHERE'S MAGNUS?
ENGINEERING. HE GOT YOUR MESSAGE. HE'S GOING TO DESTROY THIS SHIP.
COME ON! WE HAVE TO GET AWAY! NOW! BEFORE WE'RE BLOWN UP WITH IT.
ENGINEERING.
WE HAVE FIVE MINUTES. LET'S GET OUT OF HERE!
I CAN'T. I'M AUTOMATICALLY MONITORED. IF I TRY TO LEAVE ENGINEERING, AN ALARM WILL SOUND...
...AND WE DON'T WANT TO DRAW THEM HERE.
I NEVER THOUGHT I'D BE GLAD DEPLETED PERSONNEL FORCED THOSE MONSTERS TO USE A HUMAN ENGINEER.
BUT, THANKS TO YOU, IT GAVE ME THE CHANCE TO PERSONALLY CONSIGN THIS SPACE-BRIG INTO HELL!
TAKE CARE OF MY DAUGHTER.
BUT--
I DON'T MIND DYING. I JUST DON'T WANT LEEJA TO SEE ME LIKE THIS. GO!

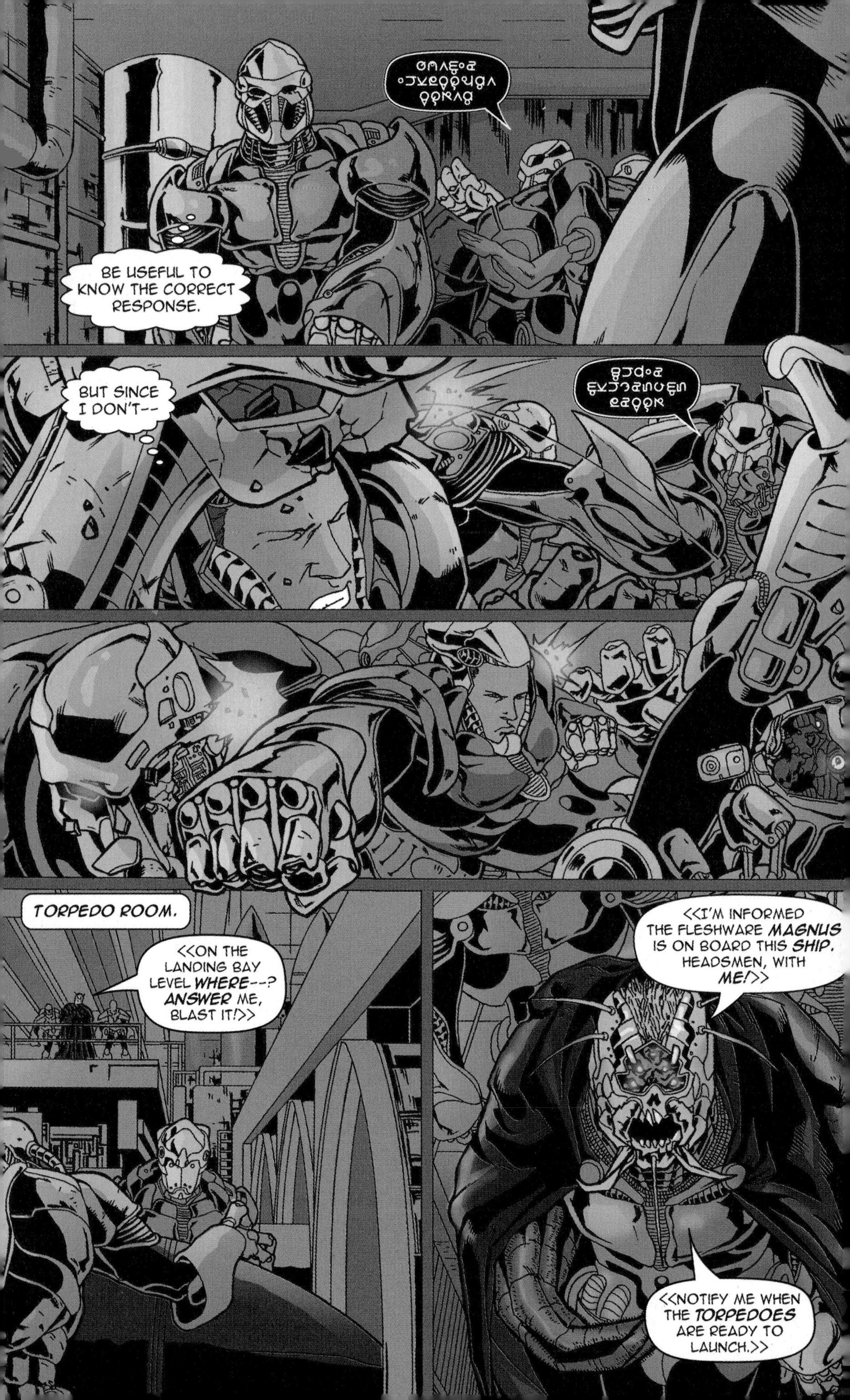
BE USEFUL TO KNOW THE CORRECT RESPONSE.
BUT SINCE I DON'T--
TORPEDO ROOM.
<<ON THE LANDING BAY LEVEL WHERE--? ANSWER ME, BLAST IT!>>
<<I'M INFORMED THE FLESHWARE MAGNUS IS ON BOARD THIS SHIP. HEADSMEN, WITH ME!>>
<<NOTIFY ME WHEN THE TORPEDOES ARE READY TO LAUNCH.>>

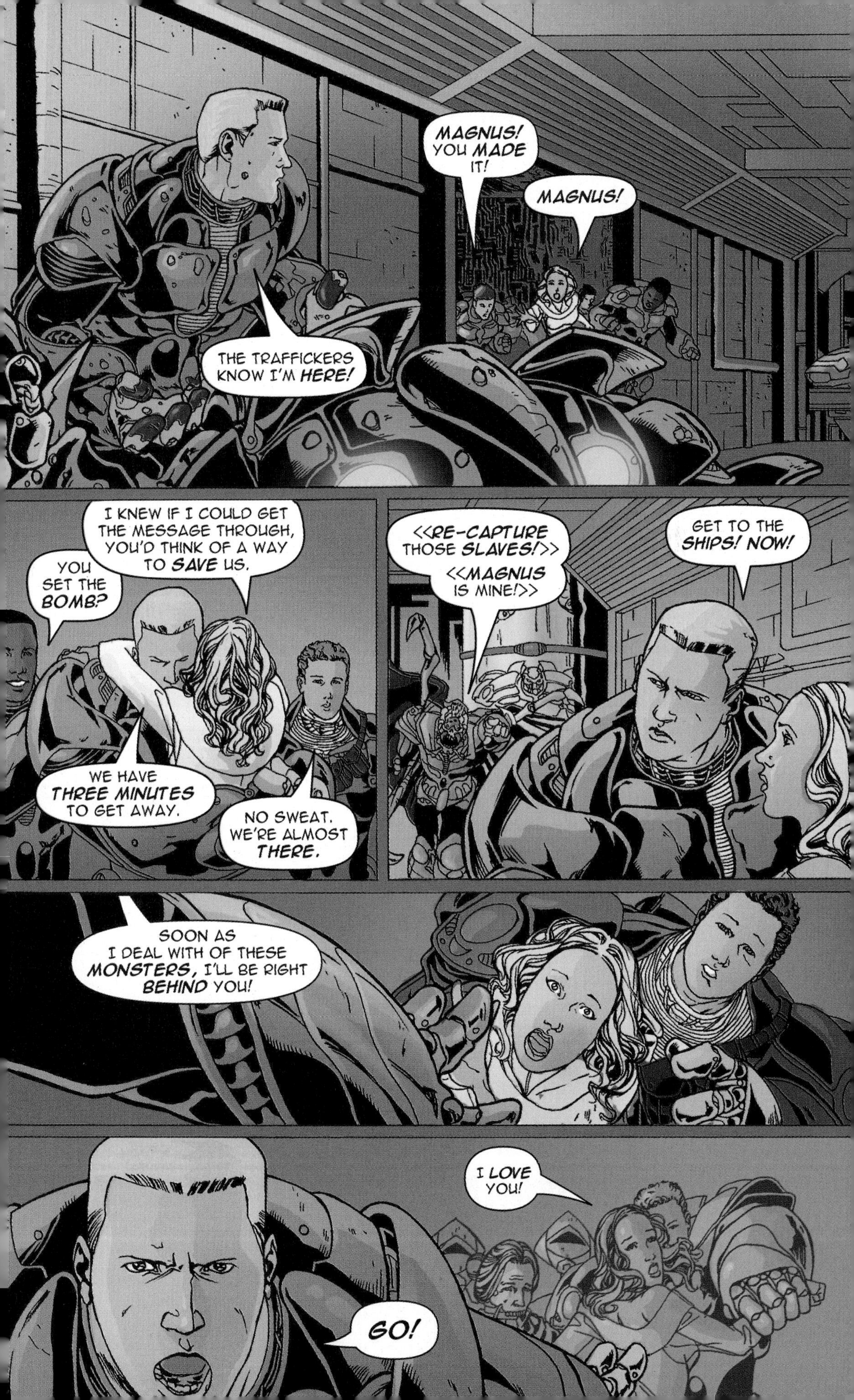
MAGNUS! YOU MADE IT!
MAGNUS!
THE TRAFFICKERS KNOW I'M HERE!
YOU SET THE BOMB?
I KNEW IF I COULD GET THE MESSAGE THROUGH, YOU'D THINK OF A WAY TO SAVE US.
WE HAVE THREE MINUTES TO GET AWAY.
NO SWEAT. WE'RE ALMOST THERE.
<<RE-CAPTURE THOSE SLAVES!>>
<<MAGNUS IS MINE!>>
GET TO THE SHIPS! NOW!
SOON AS I DEAL WITH OF THESE MONSTERS, I'LL BE RIGHT BEHIND YOU!
I LOVE YOU!
GO!

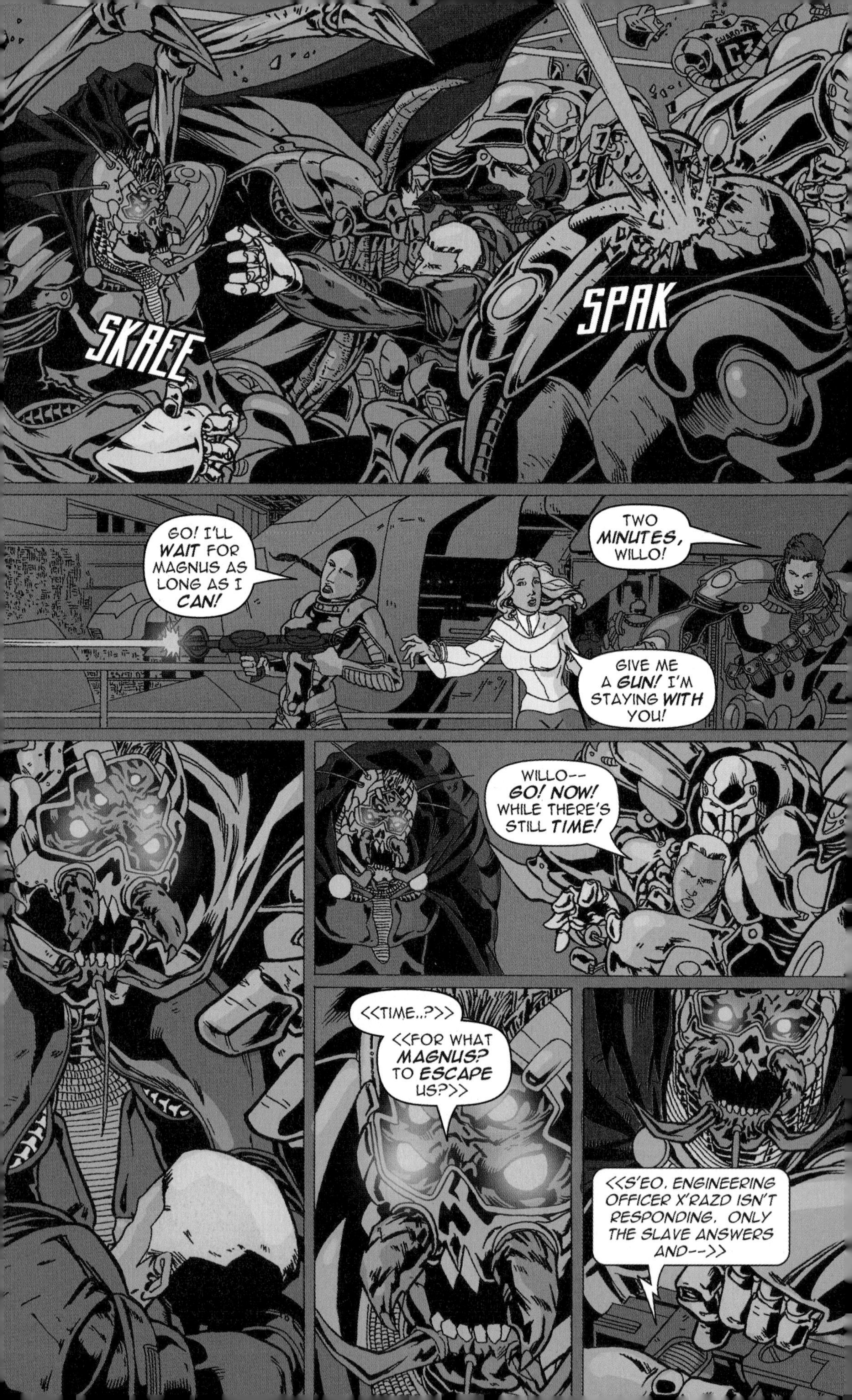
SKREE
SPAK
GO! I'LL WAIT FOR MAGNUS AS LONG AS I CAN!
TWO MINUTES, WILLO!
GIVE ME A GUN! I'M STAYING WITH YOU!
WILLO-- GO! NOW! WHILE THERE'S STILL TIME!
<<TIME..?>>
<<FOR WHAT MAGNUS? TO ESCAPE US?>>
<<S'EO. ENGINEERING OFFICER X'RAZD ISN'T RESPONDING. ONLY THE SLAVE ANSWERS AND-->>

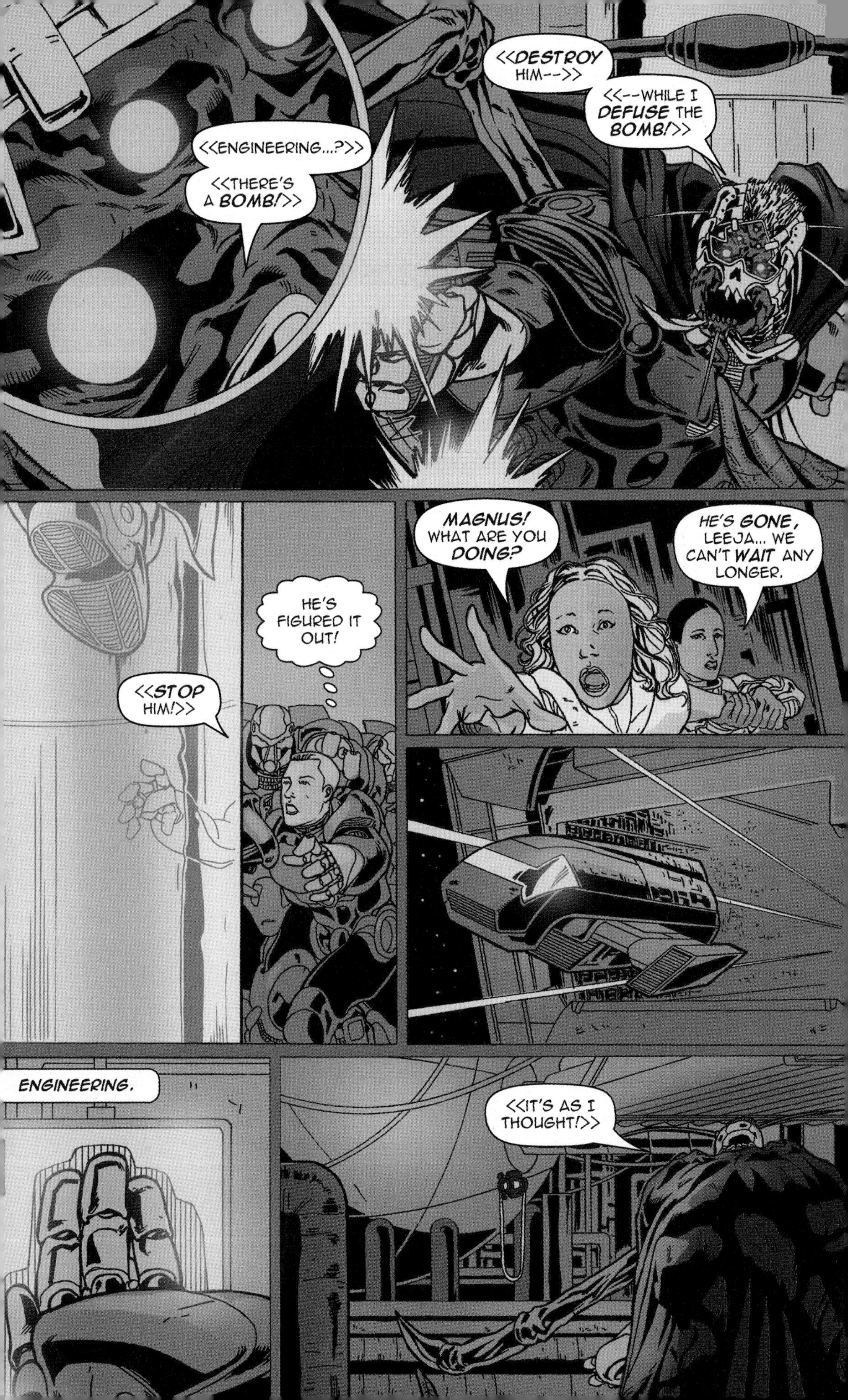

<<ENGINEERING...?>>
<<THERE'S A BOMB!>>
<<DESTROY HIM-->>
<<--WHILE I DEFUSE THE BOMB!>>
<<STOP HIM!>>
HE'S FIGURED IT OUT!
MAGNUS! WHAT ARE YOU DOING?
HE'S GONE, LEEJA... WE CAN'T WAIT ANY LONGER.
ENGINEERING.
<<IT'S AS I THOUGHT!>>

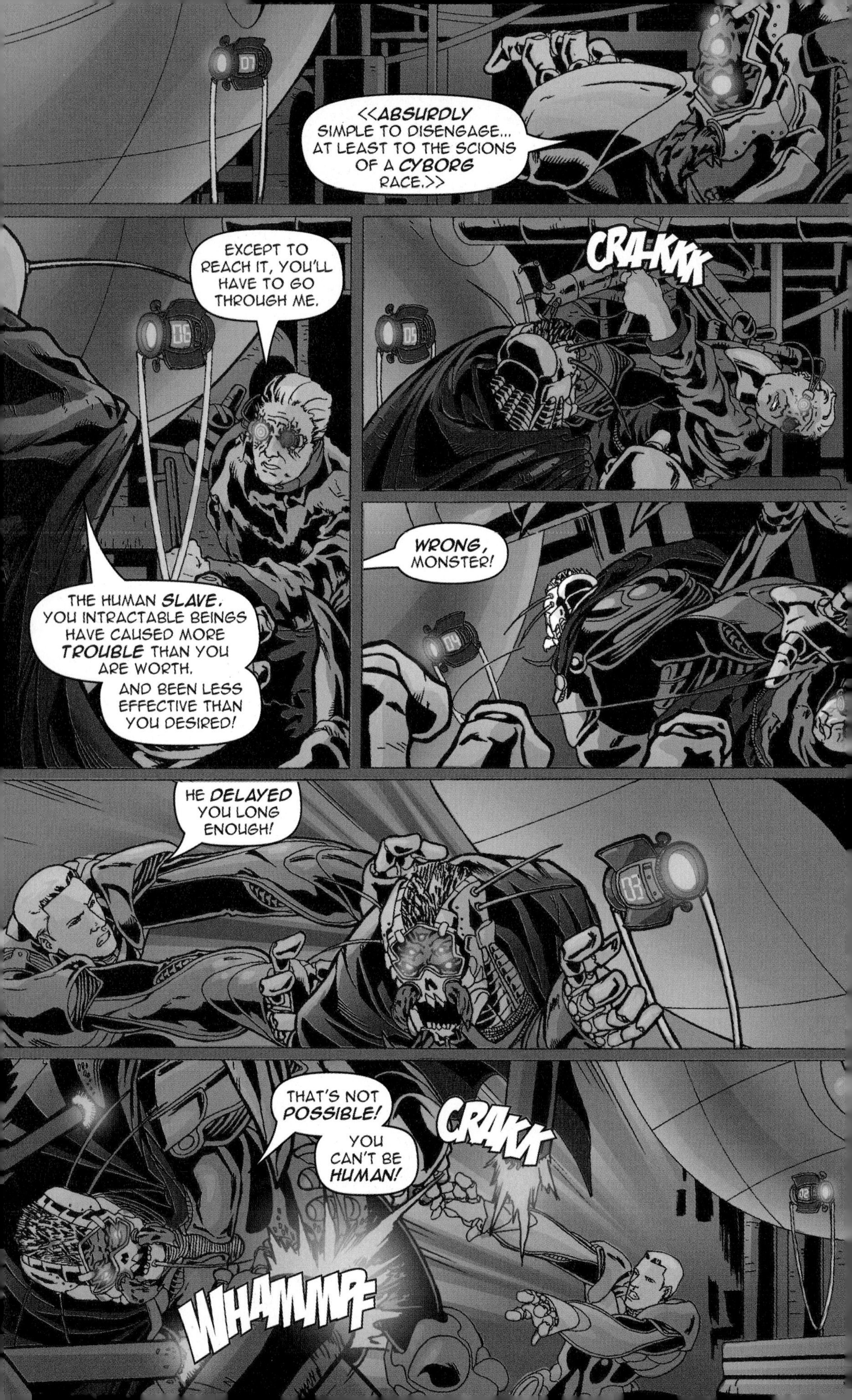
<<ABSURDLY SIMPLE TO DISENGAGE... AT LEAST TO THE SCIONS OF A CYBORG RACE.>>
EXCEPT TO REACH IT, YOU'LL HAVE TO GO THROUGH ME.
CRA-KKK
THE HUMAN SLAVE. YOU INTRACTABLE BEINGS HAVE CAUSED MORE TROUBLE THAN YOU ARE WORTH.
AND BEEN LESS EFFECTIVE THAN YOU DESIRED!
WRONG, MONSTER!
HE DELAYED YOU LONG ENOUGH!
THAT'S NOT POSSIBLE!
YOU CAN'T BE HUMAN!
CRAKK
WHAMMF

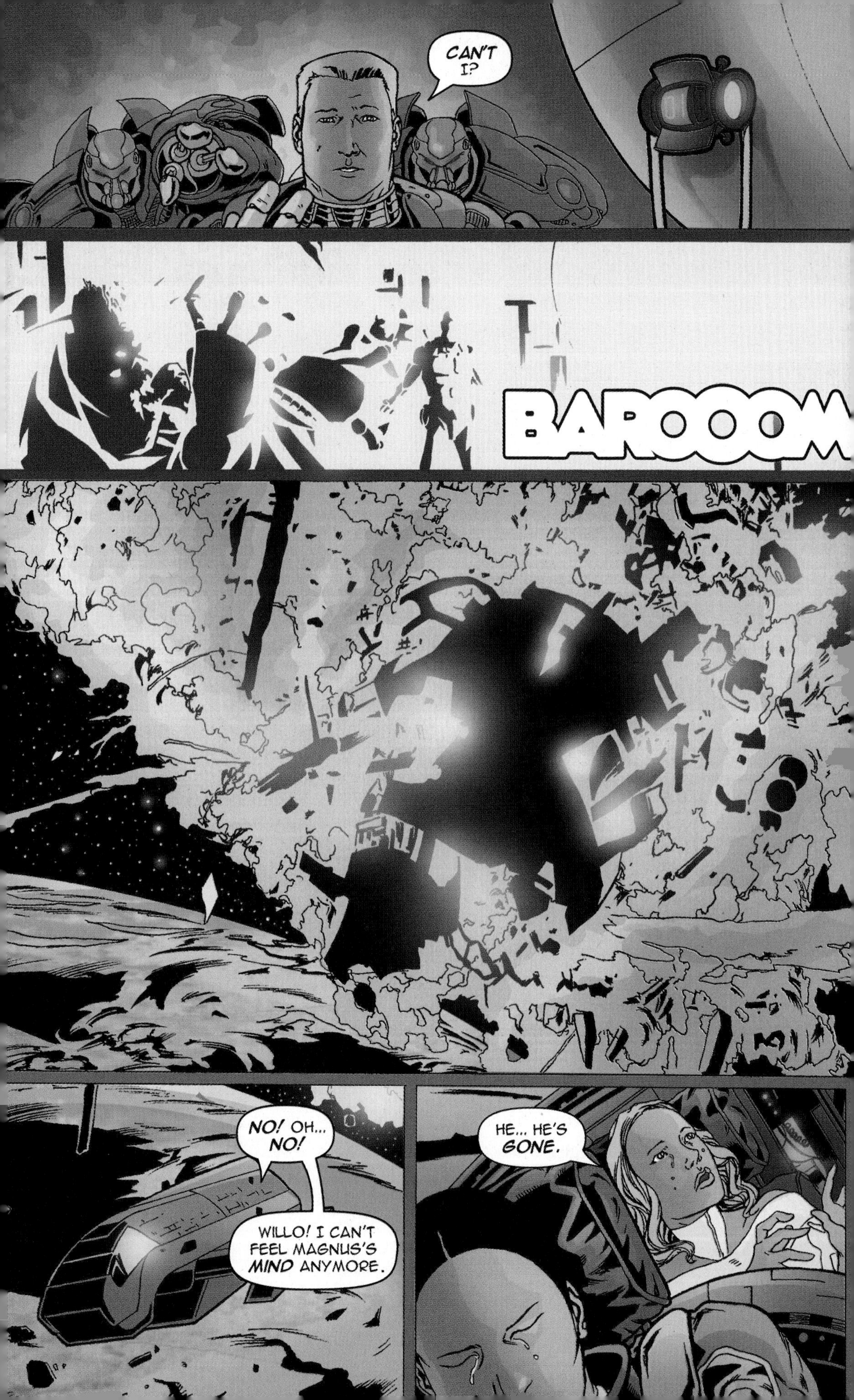
CAN'T I?
BAROOOM
NO! OH... NO!
WILLO! I CAN'T FEEL MAGNUS'S MIND ANYMORE.
HE... HE'S GONE.

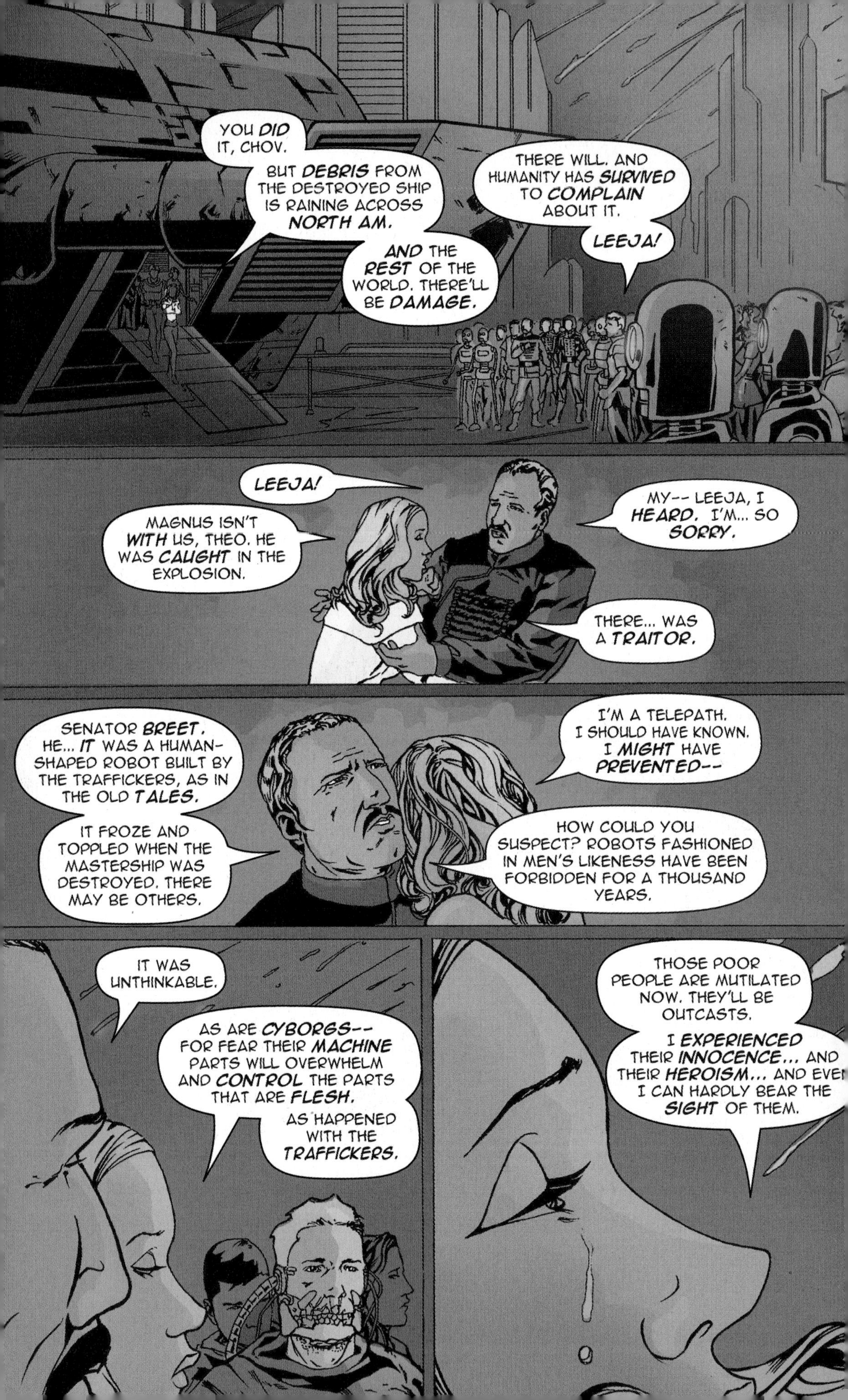
YOU DID IT, CHOV.
BUT DEBRIS FROM THE DESTROYED SHIP IS RAINING ACROSS NORTH AM.
AND THE REST OF THE WORLD. THERE'LL BE DAMAGE.
THERE WILL. AND HUMANITY HAS SURVIVED TO COMPLAIN ABOUT IT.
LEEJA!
LEEJA!
MY-- LEEJA, I HEARD. I'M... SO SORRY.
MAGNUS ISN'T WITH US, THEO. HE WAS CAUGHT IN THE EXPLOSION.
THERE... WAS A TRAITOR.
SENATOR BREET. HE... IT WAS A HUMAN-SHAPED ROBOT BUILT BY THE TRAFFICKERS, AS IN THE OLD TALES.
IT FROZE AND TOPPLED WHEN THE MASTERSHIP WAS DESTROYED. THERE MAY BE OTHERS.
I'M A TELEPATH. I SHOULD HAVE KNOWN. I MIGHT HAVE PREVENTED--
HOW COULD YOU SUSPECT? ROBOTS FASHIONED IN MEN'S LIKENESS HAVE BEEN FORBIDDEN FOR A THOUSAND YEARS.
IT WAS UNTHINKABLE.
AS ARE CYBORGS-- FOR FEAR THEIR MACHINE PARTS WILL OVERWHELM AND CONTROL THE PARTS THAT ARE FLESH.
AS HAPPENED WITH THE TRAFFICKERS.
THOSE POOR PEOPLE ARE MUTILATED NOW. THEY'LL BE OUTCASTS.
I EXPERIENCED THEIR INNOCENCE... AND THEIR HEROISM... AND EVEN I CAN HARDLY BEAR THE SIGHT OF THEM.

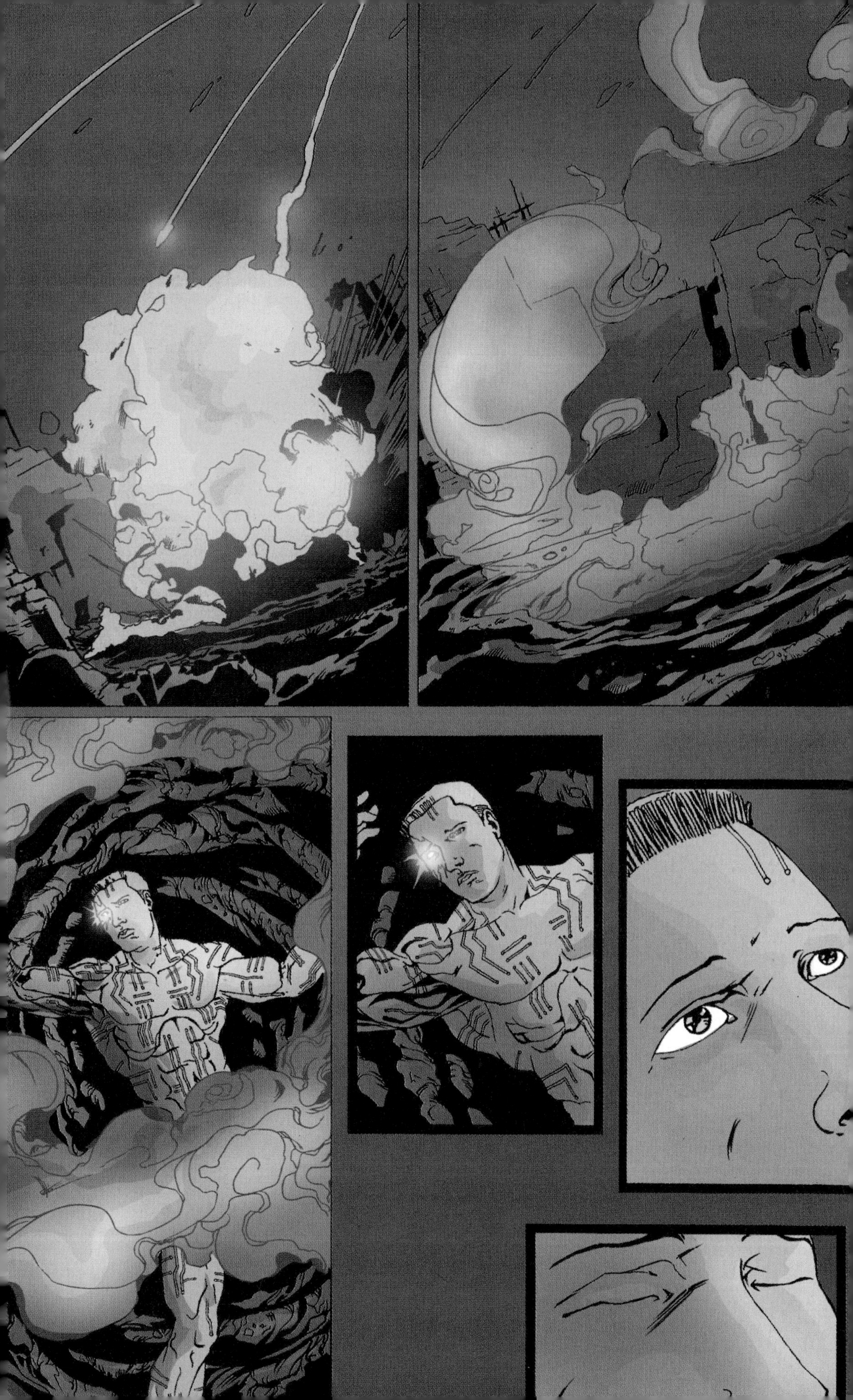

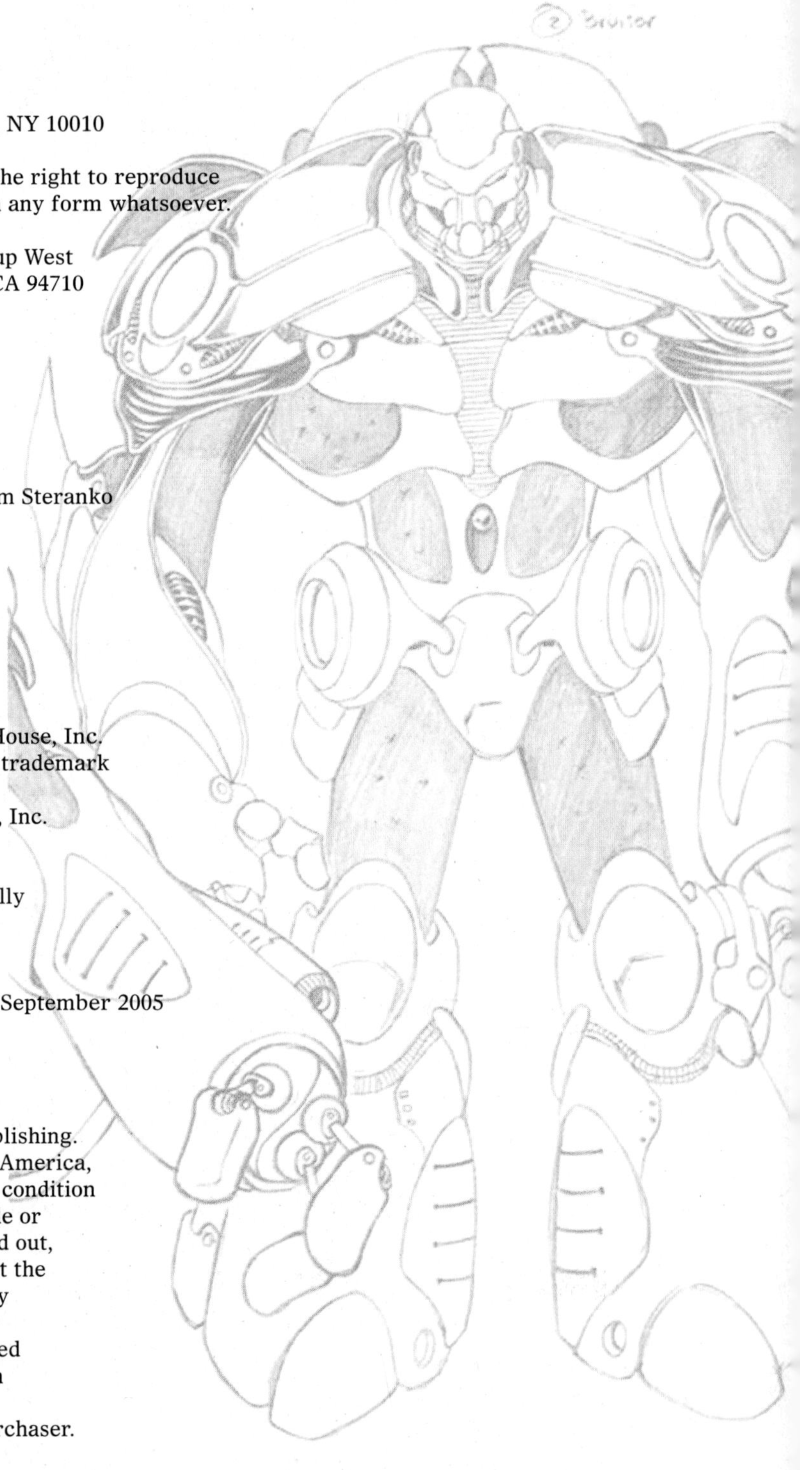

An ibooks, inc. Book
24 West 25th Street, New York, NY 10010

Distributed by Publishers Group West
1700 Fourth Street, Berkeley, CA 94710
www.pgw.com

Script: Louise Simonson
Art: Damion Hendricks
Lettering: Charles Prichett
Color: Narek Gevorgian
Cover art: John Watson
Magnus character redesign: Jim Steranko

Editor: Howard Zimmerman

Interior Design: M. Postawa
Cover art: John Watson
Cover Design: M. Postawa

Magnus Robot Fighter#1
copyright © 2005 by Random House, Inc.
Magnus Robot Fighter is a ™ trademark
of Random House, Inc.
under license to Classic Media, Inc.
All rights reserved.

Magnus, Robot Fighter originally
created by Russ Manning

First Published by ibooks, inc. September 2005
10 9 8 7 6 5 4 3 2 1

ISBN 1-59687-833-9